A Beginner's Guide
TECHNICAL ANALYSIS

Disclaimer: The information provided in this book "A Beginner's Guide to Technical Analysis" is intended for educational and informational purposes only. It is not intended to provide financial, investment, or trading advice. The content of this book is based on the author's personal opinions and experiences and should not be considered as a recommendation to buy, sell, or hold any specific financial instrument.

Trading and investing in the financial markets involve a significant level of risk and is not suitable for all investors. The author and publisher are not responsible for any losses or damages incurred as a result of using the information presented in this book. Readers should do their own research and analysis before making any investment decisions.

Furthermore, the strategies and techniques presented in this book are not guaranteed to be successful in all market conditions. Past performance is not indicative of future results. Readers should always consult with a financial advisor or professional before making any investment decisions.

In short, this book is not a substitute for professional financial advice and readers should use the information provided at their own risk.

I dedicate this book to my girlfriend who supports me through thick and thin, even when I lock myself away for weeks on end to write this book.

Three Candles Press

About Us

At Three Candles Press, we're passionate about empowering individuals to take control of their financial futures. Our mission is to provide **useful** and engaging resources that **break down** the world of investing for everyone!

Our growing team of experts and seasoned writers are working together to bring you a wide range of insightful books, guides, and articles on investing and trading.

If you want to get in touch, email us at info@threecandles.press we'd love to chat!

We hope you enjoy this book, don't forget to leave us a review!

Table of Contents

Foreword

As someone who has been involved in the financial markets for many years, there is money to be made in the markets, and there isn't only one correct answer on how to do it. Throughout the years, I went from being the typical buy and hold investor to someone who has immersed their strategy in the world of technical analysis. I strongly believe that the technical analysis discussed can be done by anyone, and I believe that once you grasp the principles and methods used, they will stick with you forever. These principles and methods can massively improve the way you invest or trade in the markets and can ultimately leave you making more informed investment decisions and more money. This, along with my joy for writing and helping others, is why I am thrilled to introduce "The Beginner's Guide to Technical Analysis".

Technical analysis is a powerful and widely used method for quickly evaluating a stock or any security, enabling traders and investors to identify patterns and trends and predict where the market may move to in the future. It provides an essential framework for making informed decisions based on historical price and volume data, rather than relying solely on intuition or guesswork. Although some may perceive this discipline as the exclusive domain for professionals, my experience has taught me that anyone, with the right guidance and dedication, can become proficient in technical analysis and make money in the markets.

This book condenses my years of expertise in the field, presenting information in a manner that is both comprehensive and approachable. Throughout the pages that follow, you will find step-by-step guides, real-world examples, and detailed explanations that will help you understand the different domains of technical analysis.

As you embark on this exciting journey, I encourage you to keep an open mind, be patient with yourself, and always strive to learn more. Success in the markets is not an overnight accomplishment, but a reward earned through dedication, hard work, and the unwavering belief that you too can achieve financial success.

With "The Beginner's Guide to Technical Analysis" in hand, I am confident that you will be well on your way to unlocking the secrets of the markets and working to build up an invaluable, equitable skillset.

Here's to your success and the incredible opportunities that await you.

All the best,
Three Candles Press

I. An Introduction To Technical Analysis

Technical analysis: a fascinating and powerful tool that has captivated the attention of countless traders and investors for decades. At its core, technical analysis is the study of historical price data and trading volume to identify trends, patterns, and potential opportunities in financial markets. By analyzing these past movements, traders can gain insights into the forces that drive market dynamics and make informed decisions about future price movements.

In a world where news and information flow faster than ever, technical analysis has emerged as a critical skill for those seeking an edge in today's competitive financial markets. Unlike fundamental analysis, which focuses on the intrinsic value of a company or asset, technical analysis is grounded in the belief that price movements are not entirely random, and that history tends to repeat itself. By uncovering recurring patterns and deciphering the psychology behind market movements, technical analysts aim to capitalize on the opportunities that arise from these predictable patterns.

In its simplest sense, technical analysis can be thought of as using data from the trading chart to make investment decisions.

The core tenets of technical analysis are:

1. **Market action discounts everything:** This principle asserts that all available information, including economic factors, market sentiment, and political events, is already reflected in an asset's price. Therefore, technical analysts focus solely on price and volume data to make their predictions.

2. **Prices move in trends:** Technical analysis is built on the premise that prices tend to move in trends, either upward (bullish), downward (bearish), or sideways (range-bound). Technical analysts aim to identify and capitalize on these trends by analyzing historical price movements.

3. **History tends to repeat itself:** The repetitive nature of price movements is attributed to market psychology and the consistent behavior of investors in response to specific events or stimuli. Technical analysts believe that historical patterns will likely recur, enabling them to forecast future price movements.

The Weatherman

To understand technical analysis, consider the analogy of weather forecasting. Meteorologists study past weather patterns and use advanced tools to analyze real-time data to predict future weather conditions. Similarly, technical analysts examine historical price and volume data to anticipate future market trends.

Just as meteorologists use various tools and techniques like satellite imagery, radar, and computer models, technical analysts employ a wide range of tools, such as chart patterns, indicators, and oscillators. Each of these tools serves a specific purpose, providing insights into different aspects of market behavior.

In both weather forecasting and technical analysis, the goal is to make informed predictions rather than exact forecasts. Neither meteorologists nor technical analysts can guarantee the accuracy of their predictions, but their insights can help improve decision-making and risk management.

The only variable that technical analysis helps us decipher is the supply and demand in the market and its product, the price movement.

Is technical analysis bulletproof?

No, technical analysis will never be perfect and there's no one single strategy or pattern that always works. There are external factors that occurs outside of technical analysis that can easily ruin a great trade.

What technical analysis will do is give you a hint at the right buy and sell points and will add conviction and confidence when making these important investment decisions.

This journey into the realm of technical analysis will provide you with the tools and knowledge needed to analyze and interpret price charts, understand market trends, and make informed trading decisions and ultimately more money. We will explore a wide range of concepts, including support and resistance levels, chart patterns, technical indicators, Dow Theory and market psychology and much, much more!

AN INTRODUCTION TO TECHNICAL ANALYSIS
KEY POINTS:

- *Technical Analysis is the analysis of supply and demand in the markets to determine price movement, and assumes all other factors are priced into the stock.*

- *Price movements are thought to form trends and patterns that repeat themselves over time.*

- *Contrasts with fundamental analysis, which is more relevant for longer-term investors. These investors can use technical analysis to better understand the markets and better time their entries and exits.*

- *Technical analysis is never 100% perfect but can give traders an edge when trading price movements.*

II. Setting Up To Trade: What You Need To Know

What Type Of Trader Will You Be?

What is your goal with trading? It is an important decision to make since it will shape what you do, we can break it down into different areas that we want to consider and decide upon before investing.

Trader vs. Investor

The trader and investor both seek to make profits from the stock market but have different goals in the way they go about it. Investors typically follow a buy-and-hold strategy, they buy stock in good companies according to their fundamentals, and they hold for years or decades until a specific goal is met. For these investors, technical analysis excels at timing your entries and exits into these stocks.

Traders enter and exit positions more frequently, ranging from seconds to months, picking up smaller but more frequent profits to try beat a buy-and-hold strategy. Traders focus on the price movement and make more extensive use of technical analysis to guide their trading decisions. Trading requires more active market participation and monitoring, and is riskier than investing, but can be more thrilling and rewarding for the right people. If you are not sure, consider the following questions!

What is your risk tolerance and what returns are you looking to make?

With higher risk tolerance comes opportunities for greater returns. Consider your financial situation and what you are willing to lose if the worst-case scenario occurs.

If you have three children and want to invest money to set them up for their future, then your risk tolerance will likely be lower than someone in their twenties with less money and less responsibilities.

How much time/effort are you able/willing to put into trading?

There are successful routes for investors who want to make returns passively without too much effort, and for investors who actively track and trade the markets and specialize in specific industries but again the best answer is whichever is the best fit for you!

Consider how much free time you could allocate to your investing or trading journey. If you are working a full-time job and have a family, day trading would likely be less viable than to someone who is on their summer break from university.

What timeframe are you looking to hold your investments?

There are no wrong answers, but the best answer will be whatever is the best fit for you! Are you investing money with the goal of making enough for a wedding at a certain date? Or with the goal of buying a new car by next year?

If you are putting money in that you will need in a year's time, then you should not be using that money to invest or trade for the long term. If you are unable to commit some time every day to monitor the trading charts, then similarly, day trading is not for you.

Choosing The Right Broker For You

Generally, the main things you will want to consider are what products the brokerages offer, what services the brokerages offer, the fees & limits associated with the brokerage and the requirements.

If you are a longer-term investor, zero-commission on buying and selling is also nice but not as essential. You may want a broker with the lowest fees possible overall, and a broad choice of products for diversification without too much concern on the breadth of services offered since you just plan to buy and hold.

If you plan to day-trade, you will be entering and exiting multiple positions during the day and so you would benefit most from a broker that offers zero-commission trading on all the securities you want to trade.

For trading, some important features you will need:

1. Trading charts with data in real-time
2. A wide range of technical indicators available
3. The ability to annotate the trading chart and save these annotations
4. To be able to create custom lists
5. To be able to fit multiple trading charts on one screen
6. To quickly switch trading charts

These are some of the questions you need to ask when choosing your brokerage. It is wise to also check reviews online regarding any potential brokers you plan to use.

The broker you choose will depend on what location you are in. Some popular brokers include Interactive Brokers, TD Ameritrade, Robinhood and eToro, each differing in the products, services, fee structure and requirements.

Alternatively, you can get all these features on a trading platform such as tradingview.com, a platform we use for charting, trading, screening, keeping up with financial news and much more. You can connect a broker to TradingView and harness the zero or low fee broker with the scope of tools that a trading platform can offer.

Once you have opened an account with a broker, get comfortable with everything first and understand where all the useful functions are.

Placing A Trade

You are now comfortable with your broker, and you now have a list of investments available for you to trade. Nowadays, buying an investment can be as simple as clicking 'buy' and specifying the quantity to purchase. However, there are some things to be aware of, as well as some useful options for traders.

Firstly, when purchasing any investment, a broker will typically quote a buy price called a bid and a sell price called an ask. They are almost always slightly different, and the difference between them is called the **bid-ask spread**. This spread is what the market takes for **providing liquidity** and is a cost of trading. Usually, the bid-ask spread is tiny and not a concern for most investments, however, some investments, particularly that of small or foreign companies, or certain derivatives that are not traded much can have very high bid-ask spreads due to their illiquidity. Subsequently, this can potentially eat into any gains on an investment and should be considered before making the investment. Indeed, liquidity for an investment can change over time – a good way to track an investment's liquidity is by looking at trends in its trading volume.

Secondly, traders have a choice when they come to buy an investment. When buying, what happens is an order is placed, and matched with a seller. The order type generally comes in two types, a market order, and a limit order.

A market order can be thought of as the automatic mode, you want to buy/sell your stock at the closest available market prices that you can instantly transact with, determined automatically. This will be the default when you one-click buy and sell anything on your broker.

Normally, the liquidity (the number of buyers/sellers) is such that orders can be executed very close to market prices, but do watch out on lesser-known investments, and always check the bid/ask spread if you are unsure.

A limit order can be thought of as the manual mode; when you want to buy/sell a stock at a price of your choosing. For example, if a stock was trading for $20, but you were only willing to pay $15 per share, you could place a limit order for $15. When the market price is $15, your orders will be automatically filled. However, if the market price never reaches $15, then the order is never executed. You can also set a duration that the limit order is there for, such as GTC (Good till cancelled).

Stop Loss & Take Profit

These two are essential risk-management tools when trading. A stop loss is used to limit your losses when trading and can be used by short-term traders and long-term investors.

When you place a trade on anything based off technical and/or fundamental analysis, it is never going to be perfect and sometimes the opposite of what you expect happens, and if so, the largest downside is that lose all your money.

To mitigate this downside, when you place a trade, you can choose to place a stop loss order at a certain price or percentage below the market price so that if this happens, your maximum downside is whatever you set the stop loss to.

With stop losses, you want to ensure that they are not too close to the current market price, as the risk if that the stock drops and triggers the stop loss before climbing to the desired price target. There is no fixed percentage for what is 'too close' but the best option is often to place it between 2-20% under depending on the stock itself (larger stocks are less volatile) and the expected price target. We will delve into where to place stop losses when we discuss trading breakouts later in this book.

Stop losses are good for managing downside risk and generally, the greater you rely on technical analysis, the more you want to be using these stop losses. There are sometimes other types of stop losses given to you by your broker, one common one is a trailing stop loss – which if you set a percentage under market price, follows your position if you are up instead of being stationary. For example, if the price of a stock went from $10 to $15 and you bought at $10 with a trailing stop loss of 10%, your stop loss would increase from $9 to $13.50.

The opposite of a stop loss is called a take profit and can be placed to automatically close part or all your position on a stock at a pre-determined price.

In Fig.1 below, a trader sees a possible trend reversal on the USD/JPY currency pair. He enters a trade at "X" where he believes the trend has reversed, and places a stop loss at 103.274, right below the previous low, and at a 0.77% loss. He expects the trade to hit at least 106.471 should the trend reversal be successful and so places a take profit here, at a 2.3% gain.

Fig. 1: *USD/JPY D1 2020-2021 (Jul-May) with take profit level and stop loss level annotated.*

The trader has made an informed decision in placing the trade and now removes any emotion from decision making during the trade, since the stop loss and take profit has been placed. The risk to reward (R/R) of the following trade is 3 since the take profit is at 3x the stop loss. The higher the R/R ratio, the better.

On this occasion, the trade was successful, and the take profit was hit, but notice how the price continues to rally after the position is closed. A trader may feel FOMO, or the urge to extend the take profit in hopes to capture more of the rally, but in doing so, begins to introduce emotion into the equation.

Both stop-losses and take profits are recommended for every trade you place, because not only do they limit your downside risk on a trade, but they also take the emotion out of the trade once a position is opened.

Asset Classes

As traders, it does not need to just be stocks that we choose to invest or trade in. Here are different assets that are available to us, with a summary of them and their features.
Remember, technical analysis methods that we have discussed in this book can be used whatever asset class you choose to trade.

- **Stocks** - Stocks represent ownership shares in a company. When investors buy stocks, they essentially become partial owners of the company and can potentially benefit from the company's growth and success via dividends that some companies pay out, and capital gains. Stocks are generally considered risk assets that have potential for higher returns but also come with higher risk. Buying stocks on most brokerages means buying the underlying stock but brokerages also offer the same companies via some sort of derivative such as futures, CFDs or option. This allows you to leverage your positions in this stock but does not mean you own the underlying stock.

- **ETFs -** ETFs stand for exchange-traded funds and are the most common way for investors and traders to purchase indices such as the S&P 500 or Dow Jones without leverage. ETFs typically hold a basket of investments, such as the underlying companies in the S&P 500 and pay out dividends from those companies, just like holding a stock. ETFs are normally diversified and lower risk than stocks. The number of ETFs available are endless, they include Gold, via the GLD ETF, almost any index you can think off, the inverse of those indices, such as the SQQQ, an inverse of the Nasdaq Composite and even Bitcoin via the BTC ETF.

- **Bonds -** Fixed income securities, or bonds, are debt instruments issued by governments, corporations, or other entities to raise capital. In exchange for lending money, bondholders receive periodic interest payments (coupon payments) and the return of the principal amount at the end of the bond's maturity. Bonds are generally considered to be less risky than stocks and offer more predictable income streams. The bonds themselves fluctuate in price and are traded on separate exchanges.

- **Commodities** - Commodities are raw materials or primary agricultural products that are traded on exchanges or in the over the counter (OTC) market. They include products like crude oil, natural gas, gold, silver, copper, wheat, corn, and soybeans. Commodities can be traded through futures contracts or ETFs. Trading commodities through futures is a feature on most online brokerages and allows traders to access leverage. Commodities are considered risk assets, and because they are primarily accessible through derivatives, are inherently riskier than buying underlying stocks. Some commodities move predictably, for example, Gold and Silver are seen as hedges during times of economic downturn, and so tend to perform well when the economy is doing badly.

- **Foreign Exchange (Forex)** - The foreign exchange market, also known as Forex or FX, is the largest and most liquid financial market globally, where currencies are traded against each other – the most popular pair being the Euro vs the U.S. Dollar (EUR/USD). Forex trading involves speculating on the relative value of one currency against another. Currency values are influenced by various factors, including interest rates, economic data, and geopolitical events. Forex trading offers traders high liquidity, 24-hour market access, and traders have access to large amounts of leverage. Forex is traded on a separate exchange to stocks, although most brokerages will integrate forex with stocks within their offerings, and when buying a forex pair, you are typically buying a derivative.

- **Cryptocurrencies** - Cryptocurrencies are digital or virtual currencies have risen in popularity over the past few years. Like forex, they come in currency pairs, such as BTC/USD and are generally traded on specialized cryptocurrency exchanges, separate from stocks. Cryptocurrencies are considered high risk, more so than stocks, meaning there is potential for big profits but also large losses. They are highly volatile and subject to regulatory risks, making them a more speculative investment option.

Using Short Selling, Derivatives & Leverage

Short selling is a trading strategy in which an investor borrows shares of a stock from a broker and sells them in the open market, with the intention of buying them back at a lower price later. If the stock price declines as anticipated, the short seller can repurchase the shares at a lower cost, return the borrowed shares to the broker, and pocket the difference as profit. However, if the stock price rises, the short seller faces potential losses, as they must repurchase the shares at a higher price to cover their position. Since short selling requires borrowing, it is inherently riskier than buying.

Short selling, or shorting in this case can also be achieved using derivatives. Using derivatives is also inherently riskier than buying underlying stock or assets, as purchasing derivatives often entails broker fees where buying the underlying may be commission free or cheaper. Derivatives are also often contracts between you and the broker, so there may be less liquidity for derivatives and therefore a higher bid-ask spread.

Derivatives also offer leverage more readily, which should be used with caution, particularly when starting out.

Leverage in today's age has become more accessible than ever. Leverage is a powerful financial tool used by traders to increase their exposure to an asset without committing the full value of the position upfront. Essentially, leverage allows traders to control larger positions using a smaller amount of capital, magnifying potential gains but also amplifying potential losses.

Leverage is typically provided by brokers, who require traders to deposit a certain percentage of the position's total value as collateral, known as the margin. The degree of leverage is expressed as a ratio, such as 10:1 or 50:1, depending on the financial instrument. Different instruments offer different leverage, with derivatives typically offering the highest leverage. Derivatives are most common in forex, commodities and optionally in stocks and indices.

The main advantage of leverage is that it can magnify potential profits. If a trader uses leverage to open a position and the market moves in their favor, their returns will be magnified by the leverage ratio. For example, if a trader opens a $10,000 position using 50:1 leverage, they will only need to commit $200 in margin. If the position earns a 5% return, the trader will gain $500, which is a 250% return on their initial margin commitment.

However, leverage also comes with significant risks. Just as leverage can magnify gains, it can also magnify losses, giving rise to its comparison to a "double-edged sword". If the market moves against a leveraged position, the trader's losses will be amplified by the leverage ratio, potentially resulting in substantial losses relative to their initial margin commitment.

If the market moves too far against a trader's leveraged position, they may receive a margin call from their broker, requiring them to deposit additional funds to maintain the position. If the trader fails to meet the margin requirements, the broker may forcibly close the position, usually resulting in a large loss for the trader.

We can only recommend first that you are fluent at trading without leverage, including risk management before you delve into leveraged trading.

SETTING UP TO TRADE: WHAT YOU NEED TO KNOW
KEY POINTS:

- *Define your trading plan before starting. Consider aspects such as the time/effort you are willing to give to trading, your financial situation, and the timeframes you wish to trade for.*

- *Find a brokerage that suits your needs. The ideal broker will depend on you as an investor.*

- *Every investment has a bid-ask spread which is difference between the buy price and sell price. The less liquid an investment, the higher the spread and the larger the cost of trading.*

- *Market orders execute at best available prices, limit orders execute at trader determined prices.*

- *Stop losses are user determined exits used to manage downside risk on trades. Take profits are user determined exits on trades.*

- *Asset classes include stocks, bonds, ETFs, futures, options, forex, and crypto and technical analysis can be applied to all.*

- *Leverage amplifies gains and losses on each trade.*

III. The Trading Chart

Head on over to the internet or your brokerage and type in any company's stock and the first trading chart you will likely see the price represented by a line graph, such as in Fig. 2.

Line Graph

Fig. 2: *Line chart of Dow Jones Industrial Average (DJI) D1 2017 (Jun-Dec)*

As a line graph, the main data you can extract from this is the price movement over a timeframe, in this case, over the final 6 months of 2017.

The line graph is a plot of price data – which is the closing price by default – and plots them on a graph of price vs time. Each plot of data is then joined together by a straight line. Often, when you view a line graph for an assets price, you will be seeing hundreds and thousands of data points and can help us visualize information about the data in question.

This display is generally sufficient for substantiating points such as the general trend, gains, and losses and here we were able to see the general bullish pattern with no significant dips.

Additionally, a line graph is great at facilitating the comparison of one set of price data with that of another. We can add another set of data points and add another price axis to make a visual comparison between two sets of price data.

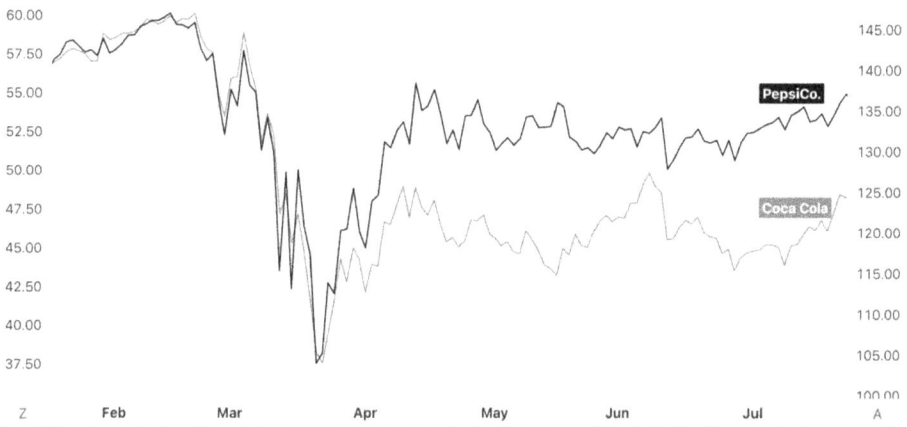

Fig. 3: *Line chart of PepsiCo. (PEP) and Coca Cola Company (KO) (Grey) D1 2020 (Jan-Jul). Price scale for PEP is located on the right, and price scale for KO is on the left.*

As we can see in Fig. 3, PEP and KO both displayed a similar trend, although after the dip in March, we can see that PEP's recovery was faster than KO, nearly reaching pre-pandemic levels by mid-April. However, KO did not manage to recover to pre-pandemic price levels by the end of July 2020. We can add more stocks and compare them all, and we can adjust the line graph to show us the % gain/loss instead of price, as shown in

Fig. 4. Here, we can see the gain/loss over time on an investment made at the start of 2020.

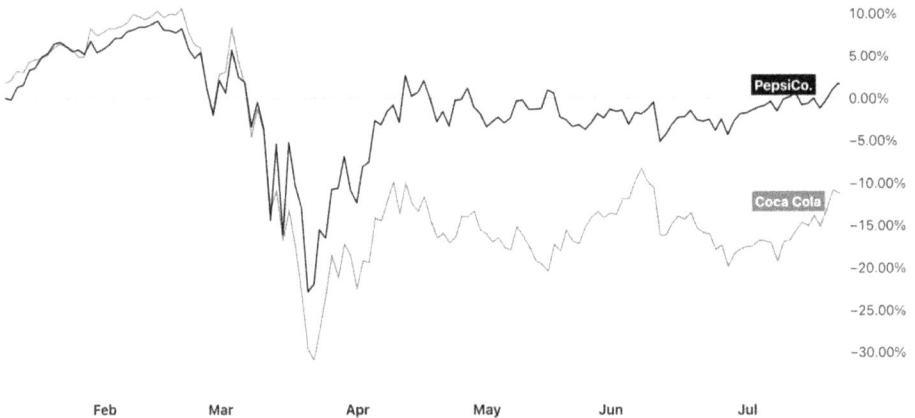

Fig. 4: *PepsiCo. (PEP) and Coca Cola Company (KO) (Grey) D1 2020 (Jan-Jul), both using the same percentage scale.*

The main limitation of the line graph is the lack of data it can display relative to charts we will discuss in a moment. If the price during a day opened at a price of $100, rallied to $120 then came back and closed at $100, we would never see that information with a line graph.

To give traders and investors a more insightful view of price action, several other charts are commonly used. The first of such charts is called the bar chart.

Bar Chart

The bar chart, different to possibly what most people first think of as a bar chart, features a continuous set of bars that contain information about a period's opening and closing prices, as well as the highest and lowest price that was reached within a period (the OHLC values). The bar chart can be used for any timeframe, where each bar will represent the timeframe chosen. A 30-minute bar chart means that each bar will represent price information every 30 minutes.

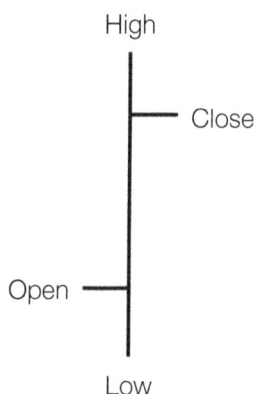

Fig. 5: *A bullish bar*

The top and bottom of the bar shows the highest and lowest price of a period respectively, and the levels show the open and close. In this bar, we can see that prices opened at a level, fluctuated below the open price (low is less than open) and eventually closed higher than the opening price, meaning this bar is bullish. Bullish bars are typically colored green, and bearish bars are typically colored red. Due to the black and white nature of this book, you will see that bullish bars are light grey, and bearish bars are dark grey.

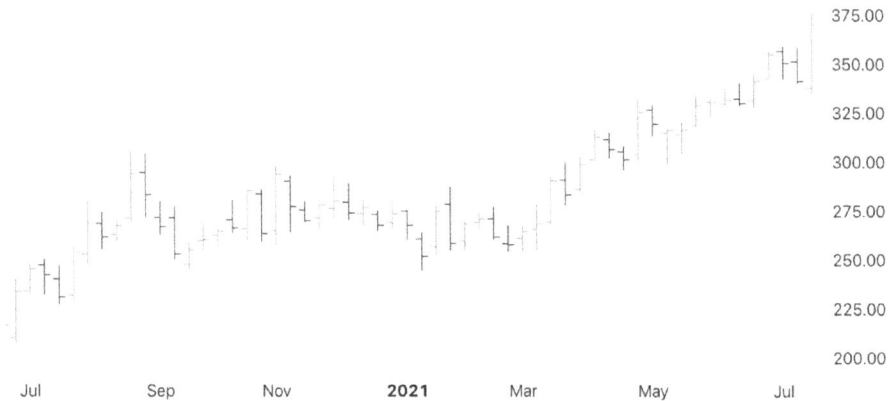

Fig. 6: *Bar chart of Meta Inc. (META) W1 2020-2021 (Jul-Jul), Facebook's parent company.*

Looking at Fig. 6, we can see that the chart shows the price opening the week in July 2020 somewhere around $210 and closing the week in July 2021 at around $370. For a one-year period, where each bar is a week, you can see the stock has done well. There is a clear trajectory where the market price for the stock goes from the bottom left to the peak in July, and we can say that this period was bullish for META.

We can also interpret specific areas within the year that were more bullish than others, and we can interpret single bars within the context of the chart.

Candlestick Chart

Expanding on the benefits of the bar chart, the candlestick chart features banister-looking blocks which are called candles or candlesticks. The central line on the bar chart is replaced with a thick body, which allows the candle to more contrastingly illustrate whether a period was bullish or bearish. Every candlestick on a chart represents a selected period of time. For example, in a 1-day trading chart, each candlestick would represent 1 day.

The candlestick is first formed at the opening price in that period. The closing price's difference to the opening price forms the body of the candlestick. If the closing price is less than the opening price, then the candlestick body will be red, if the closing price is more than the opening price, than the candlestick body will be green. If the opening price is roughly identical to the closing price, you will see a body that looks like a line – this is called a doji. The wicks above and below every candlestick represent the absolute highest and lowest market price in that given time frame.

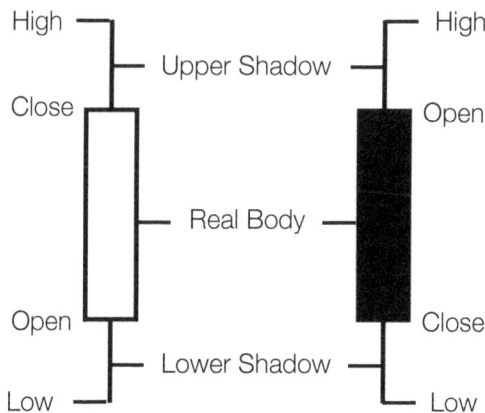

Fig. 7: *Annotated bullish candlestick (left) and a bearish candlestick (right)*

Because of the black and white nature of this book, green bullish candles are represented by white candles with a black border, and red bearish candles are represented by black candles.

Candlesticks can tell us about the momentum in a trend and the relation between buyers and sellers. A few guidelines for candlesticks:

- The larger the body of the candle, the higher the momentum.
- Candles with small bodies and large wicks, such as dojis, indicate a battle between buyers and sellers. On their own, they are neutral but given a context, may indicate a trend reversal, as we will discuss in candlestick patterns.
- A bearish candle with no lower wick, or a bullish candle with no upper wick shows strong bearish or bullish momentum respectively.

The candlestick trading chart is just tens and hundreds of these candlesticks simultaneously placed onto a graph, and the result is a chart that looks something like Fig. 8.

Fig. 8: *Candlestick chart of Meta Inc. (META) W1 2020-2021 (Jul-Jul), Facebook's parent company.*

The price data on this chart is identical to the previous bar chart, the only difference is the charting method. The same information is given, and the same interpretations can be made as with the bar chart but note how visually easier it is to interpret bullish and bearish moves. For example, we can see with ease that META had a 4-week bullish streak in March 2021, followed by a moderately bearish week following the streak.

Technical analysis can be done on any timeframe. Fig. 8 is a 1-week chart for META, but we can change it to a 1-day chart, and this will pull up a completely new set of candlesticks. We can even look at a 1-minute chart where you can see micro price movements that would otherwise be missed.

Reading the trading chart is the first step into extracting information about how the markets are affected by different parameters – and thus helps you understand the markets relationship with supply and demand. Beyond showing price information within a given timeframe, the candlestick chart can show the behavior of market participants, and candlestick patterns relating to this behavior tend to recur and predict future price movements to varying degrees of accuracy.

The candlestick chart will be the chart that we will focus on throughout this book, although there are a few other charts that are useful to know about. The first is the Heikin-Ashi, a close derivative of the candlestick chart that depicts candles according to a different formula from the regular candlestick chart.

The Heikin-Ashi chart uses the same visual representation of price data as the candlestick chart, but the calculation for the open-high-low-close (OHLC) values are different.

- Heikin-Ashi Open: The opening price of a Heikin-Ashi candle is calculated as the average of the open and close prices of the previous candle.
- Heikin-Ashi Close: The closing price is determined by taking the average of the open, high, low, and close prices of the current period.
- Heikin-Ashi High: The highest value among the current period's high, open, and close prices.
- Heikin-Ashi Low: The lowest value among the current period's low, open, and close prices.

The primary advantage of using Heikin-Ashi charts lie in their ability to filter out market noise and provide a clearer visual representation of the prevailing trend.

Fig. 9: *Heikin-Ashi chart of Meta Inc. (META) W1 2020-2021 (Jul-Jul)*

Note how price movements are smoothed compared to the candlestick chart display earlier – there are fewer alternating bullish bearish candles compared to META in Fig. 8 and the trend is easier seen.

The Logarithmic Scale

Every trading chart constructed to this point has been using the arithmetic scaling. The chart is scaled where price values are arithmetically distanced apart. For example, the distance between 100 and 110 would be the same as 110 and 120. However, on a logarithmic chart, the chart is scaled logarithmically, where the value distance is based on a percentage rather than a number. A 10% increase is represented by the same distance, so 100 and 110 would be the same as 110 to 121. The result of the log scale chart is that price data is displayed more proportionately and more logically for an investor, since a 20% price move is a 20% price move, regardless of the price.

Additionally, on shorter timeframes, the differences are minimal, but on longer timeframes, the difference become notable.

Fig. 10: *Tesla Inc. (TSLA) W1 2018-2021 displayed with arithmetic scaling (line) and logarithmic scaling (candles).*

When there is a large difference in price over a timeframe, the logarithmic scale displays price data more proportionately. Notice how price data on the arithmetic scale up until 2020 is completely dwarfed by the uptrend in 2020-2021, but a lot more information on this period before 2020 is visible on the logarithmic scale.

The logarithmic scale does come with limitations, such that it is unable to display price data well if an asset price becomes negative. Crude Oil for example went negative on the 20th April 2020, before quickly coming back to positive pricing intraday. Note in this example, the arithmetic scaling would have more reasonably displayed price data. Negative price data is a rarity, as stocks are unable to have a value of less than $0, but nonetheless, the example below illustrates the need for an investor to consider whether the chart scaling represents the price data fairly.

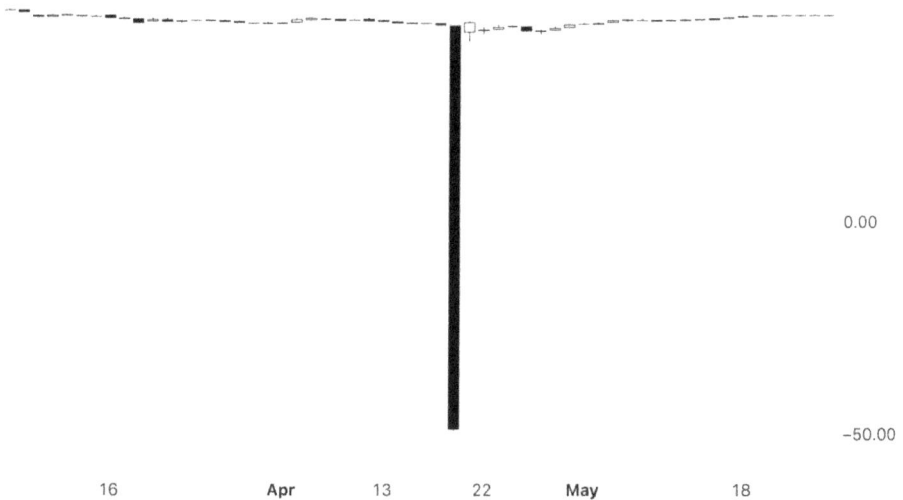

Fig. 11: *Crude Oil (CL) D1 2020 (Mar-May). The trading day on April 20th is disproportionately displayed on the logarithmic scale.*

KEY POINTS:

- Line charts give an overview of price movement and trend over time but lack OHLC (open-high-low-close) information which limit their usefulness in trading.

- Bar charts incorporates OHLC values into a vertical line, its length determined by high and low price, followed by horizontal line on the left (the opening price) and a horizonal line to the right (the closing price)

- Candlestick chart displays the same information as a bar chart, but its design makes it easier to display bullish and bearish periods. It is the charting method used throughout the book.

- Heikin-Ashi is a smoothed version of the candlestick chart.

- Arithmetic scaling makes price equidistant at a given numerical interval, logarithmic scaling makes price equidistant at a given percentage interval. Over longer timeframes, logarithmic scaling shows price action more proportionately.

IV. The Trend

No matter how the price of the stock moves over a timeframe, it's always following some type of trend. The price movement of any asset or security essentially has three options, to move in a general upwards (bullish) direction, to move in a general sideways direction or to move in a general downwards direction (bearish). In each case, the price movement over the timeframe is following a trend.

Determining the trend is the first and most crucial step for any investors and traders to make, since the trend is our friend.

If the price is headed in a bearish trend, then unless there is technical proof that a trend reversal should take place soon, then we should assume that the bearish trend will continue. If we were at a horse race, and horse number 1 was in first place and galloping faster than the other horses, it would be silly to place a bet on a horse other than horse 1 to win without good reason to do so. If the markets are moving down, then the most logical bets would be placed on markets going down further, unless technical suggest otherwise. The same is true for a bullish or sideways trend.

Technical analysis encompasses a plethora of readily available tools for any investor to use and assess the markets. Candlestick patterns, price patterns and technical indicators, all talked about in later chapters of this book, can all be used as clues as to whether the trend will last or whether a change of trend is imminent, and indeed, when the trend has changed.

Back to the horse analogy, if you analyzed horse number 1, who is the fastest, but also found that the rate of speed was negative (slowing down), then you might have reason to believe the victor of the races is to be challenged.

Trends in the markets can come in different time frames, from the longest trends being secular trends that provide a long-term bias on stocks to short term trends that last a few minutes. The technical analysis spoken about in this book can be used to determine trends on any timeframe, whether on a 1-minute chart or a 1-month chart, but trends that take place over a longer timeframe typically tend to have more technical significance once reversed or changed than smaller timeframe trends.

One of the most common theories regarding trend determination in the markets in the Dow Theory.

The Dow Theory

The Dow Theory is a technical analysis approach to stock market investing that was developed by Charles Dow, the co-founder of Dow Jones & Company, in the late 19th century. The Dow Theory is based on the premise that the stock market reflects the overall health of the economy, and that stock prices move in trends that can be analyzed and predicted using technical analysis methods.

The market is in an upward trend when a major average, such as the Dow Jones Industrial Average (DJIA) makes a higher high, confirmed by another major average also making a higher high – traditionally the Dow Jones Transportation Average (DJTA).

The Dow Theory is based on six basic principles:

1. The market discounts everything.

The stock market reflects all available information, including economic, political, and financial factors – the fundamental assumption in technical analysis. This is known as the Efficient Market Hypothesis (EMH) which we will discuss later.

2. There are three trends.

The stock market moves in three trends: the primary trend, which is a bull market or bear market that typically lasts a few months or longer. Within the bull or bear market is a temporary pullback or rally respectively, which forms the secondary trend, that typically lasts between a few weeks to a few months, and within the secondary trend is minor fluctuations that last between a few days and a few weeks that form the minor trend.

Fig. 12: *Dow Jones Industrial Average (DJI) D1 2021–2022 (Dec-Nov), with the primary trend (dark grey), intermediate trend (grey) and minor trend (light grey) annotated.*

The downtrend in U.S. equities throughout 2022, shown in Fig. 12, nicely shows the three trends in play.

3. The primary trend is the most important and has three phases.

Dow Theory suggests that primary trends consist of three distinct phases: accumulation, public participation, and distribution. The accumulation phase is when informed investors begin to buy or sell, anticipating the upcoming trend. The public participation phase is when the broader market starts to follow the trend, resulting in increased trading volume. Finally, the distribution phase is when informed investors start to exit their positions, leading to a reversal of the trend. The volume is very revealing here as institutional volume tends to be larger than retail volume, and therefore accumulation tend to have higher volumes than public participation and distribution.

4. The trend is confirmed by volume.

Trading volume should increase in the direction of the primary trend. In an uptrend, volume should increase as prices rise, and decrease during price retracements. Conversely, in a downtrend, volume should increase as prices fall, and decrease during rallies. A divergence between price trends and trading volume can signal a potential trend reversal.

Fig. 13: *Apple Inc. (AAPL) D1 2014 (May-Aug) with the volume applied and the price-volume annotated.*

In Fig. 13, volume increases as price increases, indicating a healthy bullish trend.

5. Dow Theory relies on the confirmation of both the Dow Jones Industrial Average (DJIA) and the Dow Jones Transportation Average (DJTA).

For a trend to be considered valid, both averages must reach new highs or lows in unison. For example, if the DJIA reaches a new high, but the DJTA fails to do so, the theory suggests that the primary trend may not be as strong as it initially appears.

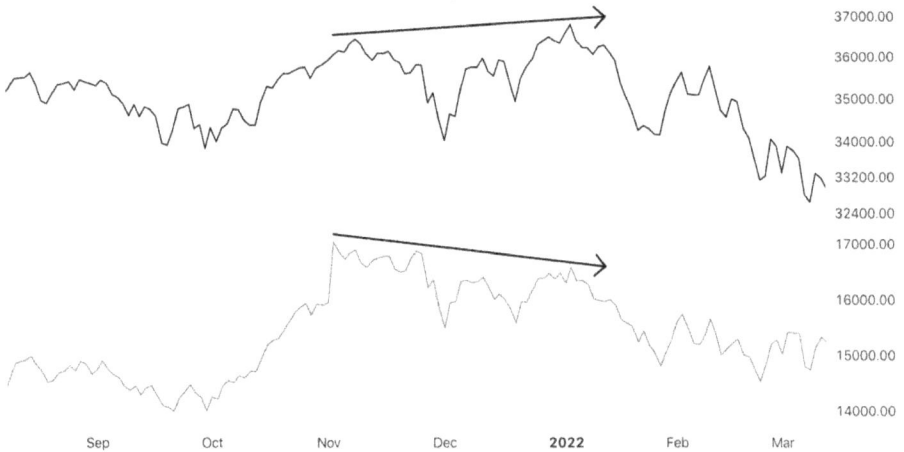

Fig. 14: *Dow Jones Industrial Average (DJI) in black and Dow Jones Transportation Average (DJT) D1 2021–2022 (Aug-Mar) with the divergence annotated.*

In Fig. 14, the DJI and the DJT both make a high at the beginning of November, followed by a pullback. The DJI then proceeds to make a higher high, peaking at the beginning of 2022, but the DJT fails to make a higher high in the same timeframe. This divergence between the DJI and DJT shows that the bull market that prevailed throughout 2021 may be coming to an end, and indeed should be a red flag for any investor or trader looking to buy or long at this point.

6. Trends continue until there is a clear reversal.

Trends in the market will continue until there is a clear reversal, indicated by a significant change in trend direction.

Trend Reversals

The most common understanding on the Dow Theory's final rule on trend reversals, is to use peak and trough analysis to identify trend reversals.

Peak and trough analysis is a widely used technique in technical analysis to identify trend reversals by analyzing the highs and lows in price movements. This method is based on the concept that price trends are a series of peaks (highs) and troughs (lows) that, when analyzed, can indicate the direction of the market and potential trend reversals.

To start, you need to identify the peaks and troughs on a price chart. A peak is a high point in the price movement, while a trough is a low point.

Once you have identified the peaks and troughs, you can determine the trend by analyzing the sequence of these points. In an uptrend, prices form higher peaks and higher troughs, while in a downtrend, prices form lower peaks and lower troughs. A sideways or range-bound trend occurs when prices form roughly equal peaks and troughs.

Fig. 15: *Barclays (BARC) W1 2004–2007 (May-Dec), with the intermediate trend highs and lows annotated, and possible trend reversal confirmations (dotted lines at A and B).*

Trend reversals can be identified when there is a change in the sequence of peaks and troughs. In a bull market, the price must make higher highs and higher lows in the intermediate trend. The price rallies from the first low to the first high, before there is a pullback. This pullback must not fall below the first low, and in not doing so, creates a higher low. The price then rallies from the higher low to a price level higher than the previous high. This succession of higher highs and higher lows confirms the continuation of the bullish trend. The moment the price drops below a previously established low, such as that labelled "A" in Fig. 15, is the moment the bullish trend may no longer intact and that a trend reversal may be taking place.

We can use technical indicators to confirm this trend reversal, chiefly the volume, as described in the Dow Theory. Recall that volume increases in the direction of the trend, and so to confirm the possible trend reversal at point "A" in BARC, we would want to see increasing volume as the price declines.

Fig. 16. *Barclays (BARC) W1 2004–2007 (May-Dec), with the volume applied, price-volume divergence annotated and possible trend reversal confirmations (dotted lines at A and B).*

Alas, the volume reveals a telling story regarding the trend. The volume clearly increases as price declines, showing what is known as a bearish divergence, and confirming that the lower low is the beginning of a new bear market.

Should the volume or other indicators not confirm a trend reversal at point "A", wait for a lower low followed by a lower high, confirmed at point "B" – where price creates a lower high and drops below the previous low – can be used as the definitive confirmation of a trend reversal.

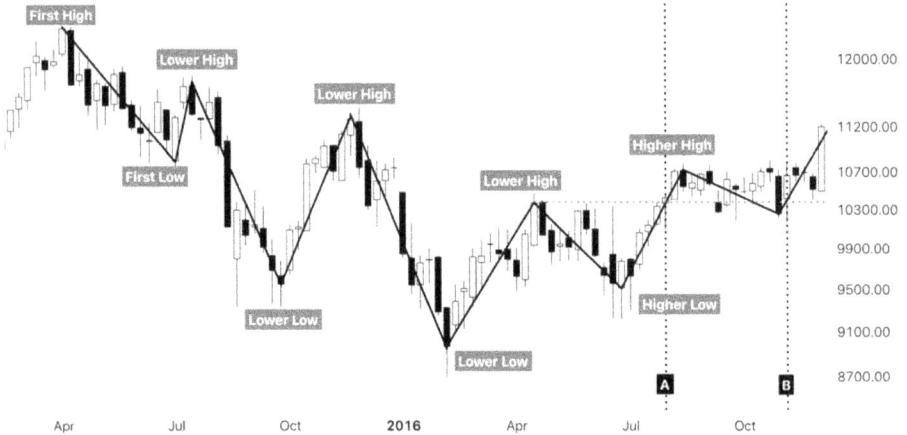

Fig. 17: *DAX Index (DEU40) W1 2015–2016 (Mar-Dec), with the intermediate trend highs and lows annotated, and possible trend reversal confirmations (dotted lines at A and B).*

The exact opposite is true for a bear market. In a bear market, the price must make lower lows and lower highs in the intermediate trend. The price declines from the first high to the first low, before there is a rally. This rally must not pass the first high, and in not doing so, creates a lower high. The price then declines from the lower high to a price level low than the previous low. This succession of lower lows and lower highs confirms the continuation of the bearish trend.

The trend reversal can be detected when the price makes a higher low, then rallies to create a higher high, triggered at point "A" where price exceeds the previous high.

Trendlines

A trendline is a line drawn on a trading chart to visually identify trends in price movement and hence guide trading activity. Use of these trendlines is incredibly versatile, as you will see later, and can help us quickly and efficiently define a technical picture. Trendlines and all the patterns discussed work for any timeframe, whether you are looking at a 1-week chart or a 1-minute chart and is relevant whichever asset class you are looking at.

Generally, the longer the timeframe of the trendline, the more significant it is (and any subsequent price breakout).

Drawing a trendline involves connecting the low points of the price to form the line of support or the high points to form the line of resistance. The line can be drawn between 2 or more of these points, where the more points there are on the trendline, the stronger the level of support or resistance is.

A line of support shows traders the level that the market price will not likely fall under when following the current trend, whereas the line of resistance shows traders the level that the market price will not likely break through when following the current trend. If the price breaks above a line of resistance or falls under line of support, this could indicate that there is a change of trend.

In Fig. 18, a trendline connecting the lows on SPX goes in an upwards direction. The trendline visually shows investors the bullish trend, and although it may seem obvious even without a trendline, when retroactively investing, no one can predict how long a trend will last. Note that during 2020-2021, the price bounces of the trendline on 7 different occasions whilst in a bull market. Each time, the trendline supports the price, and the price continues upwards. Without the trendline, how could an investor know - at the time - whether the price drop was a correction in a bullish trend, or the start of a new bearish trend?

In January 2022, the price broke decisively below the support trendline, with the largest bearish weekly candle in over a year, marking the end of the long-term bullish trend and the commencement of a new, bearish trend.

Fig. 18. *S&P 500 Index (SPX) W1 2020–2022 (Jun-Jun), with the line of support annotated and arrows pointing to the general trend. Tests of the trendline are circled in light grey, and a trendline break circled in dark grey.*

Fig. 19. *A price channel with trendlines and tests annotated.*

When the price of an asset moves in between a line of support and a line of resistance that are roughly parallel, the asset is said to be trading in a channel, or a price channel. These price channels can be bullish, bearish, or sideways, and in the same way that a trendline break (such as that demonstrated in Fig. 18) can signify a change of trend, a breakout from a price channel can also signify a change of trend.

In Fig. 20, AAL is following a bearish trend bound by a down trending channel. At the end of March, we see the price break through the resistance of the down trending channel and begin to follow an up-trending channel. A possible entry point into AAL would have been when the price broke above the down trending channel, and a possible exit is when the price breaks down from the up-trending channel.

Fig. 20: *American Airlines Group Inc. (AAL) H1 2019 (Mar-Apr). Two sets of lines of support and resistance have been added.*

These trendlines can also act as a temporary level of support or resistance in a bearish or bullish trend respectively.

Fig. 21: *NIO Inc. (NIO) D1 2021-2022 (Nov-Feb) with the line of support annotated and tests circled.*

The temporary trendlines, when broken, signal the resumption of the trend, and often, these trendlines can form price patterns that give us a price target. Keep a close eye however, as these trendlines may also signal a trend reversal via particular chart patterns, as we will see later in the book.

Broken trendlines also can reverse roles for the future price. As in the example above, the trendline supported the price in a downtrend before being broken. Extending the trendline to encompass future price data, the same line of support may present itself as a future line of resistance when prices go back up.

Fig. 22: *Foot Locker Inc. (FL) W1 2021-2023 (Oct-Mar), with the trendline in grey annotated.*

In Fig. 22, a downtrend is seen at the beginning, with a temporary halt of the downtrend, supported by the line of support at $39.89. The downtrend resumes after a decisive trendline break, pushing prices down to a low of roughly $25, followed by a trend reversal to the upside. Extending this trendline shows a level where the price on the uptrend may find some resistance. Indeed, in August 2022, the price shoots up and finds resistance by the trendline at $39.89. The price gets rejected at the trendline, retraces a small amount, and retests the trendline before a more substantial breakdown to $31. From there, the price comes to test the $39.89 trendline twice more, before finally breaking through $39.89 decisively with a large bullish weekly candle. As of March 2023, FL has come down to test $39.89 as a support, bouncing up and remaining above… for now.

An important factor here is that the price of FL is creating higher lows from its move up from $25, which gives us the idea that this price level is a temporary pause in an uptrend. Furthermore, the higher lows can be connected by a bullish facing trendline, which creates a price pattern that we will cover in a later part of this book.

Another important way for investors and traders to use the trendline is by identifying absolute support and resistance levels that have been tested on a very long-term period, typically a year or more. If an absolute support is established, it could be a level where the stock is deemed undervalued and generally a good buy by traders and investors, and therefore the target for limit orders, which execute when the price hits this level.

Practically, this would be zooming out to a high-timeframe and assessing whether price is respecting any long-term trendlines.

Fig. 23: *Tesla Inc. (TSLA) Mo1 2013-2020 with the line of support annotated and retests circled.*

Looking at TSLA on a multi-year timeframe, there is a clear line of support at the $11.93 point where the line has been tested five times in total. In each one circled in Fig. 23, the price has come down to the support line, tested it, bounced off and followed a new short-term bullish trend.

During the period in 2016, the price fell below this support level, but recovers within the month – indicative of TSLA stock being a great buy in that price range for investors, regardless of conditions.

This temporary drop below this trendline illustrates two further important points, one is that trendlines are never 100% perfect, as demonstrated, and two is that when you come to construct your trendlines, they do not need to be perfect to a T. Trendlines can encompass a general trend where a few candle wicks are intersected, or even outlier price data, if you believe it fits the overall data better.

Fig. 24: *US500 (an S&P 500 derivative) D1 2022 (Sep-Dec). The used trendlines are colored solid and the outlier price data is circled.*

In Fig. 24, the price is generally heading in a bullish direction bound by two bullish trendlines. Note how they are not perfect but suit the price data better than the alternative (dashed line). The line of support currently encompasses at least 5 price lows, but the dashed line of support, which accounts for the long October 13th wick, only encompasses 2 price lows. The two solid trendlines form a rising wedge price pattern (discussed later), and when broken, provide a price target for investors and traders that was met – unlike the equivalent price target formed from a rising wedge based on the dashed trendline.

Generally, a trendline that encompasses more of the price data is more reliable, but the alternative trendline should not be ruled out, as future price data could end up using the less regarded trendline.

Trendlines are great for highlighting areas of support and resistance, but often, the discrepancy of price lows and highs does not conform to a single trendline. Sometimes, a better way to forecast potential areas of support and resistance is to draw two trendlines that create an area between them, called a zone of support or zone of resistance. The zone of support/resistance then becomes a price range that has historically been tested multiple times.

This zone of support/resistance rules out the need for us to decide which of several trendlines is correct and gives us a general area where we could expect a potential price target in an uptrend or downtrend.

In Fig. 25, over the past five years, the JPM price has tested the zone of support many times, and therefore, we can use this zone as a potential buy signal if the price is trading above and falls to this zone or as a potential sell signal if the price is trading below and rises to this zone.

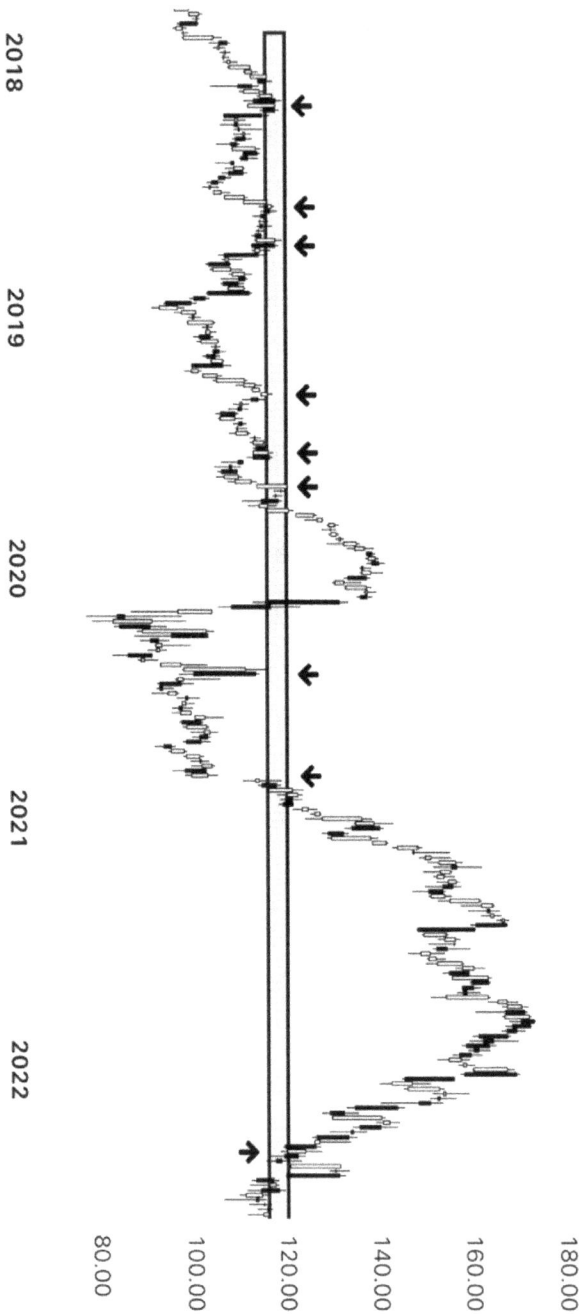

Fig. 25: *J.P. Morgan Chase (JPM) W1 2018-2022 (Jan-Jun). Two trendlines have been added at $116 and $120, and area between them shaded to indicate the zone of support.*

Drawing trendlines is a retroactive process, and so far, we have annotated trendlines retrospectively on the charts.

The trendlines don't need to be 100% accurate when drawn on the chart, the line can pass through with some margin of error – just remember this when looking for trend reversals, you will want to see a reasonable clearance through a support or resistance before buying/selling – we will discuss this in the Trading Breakouts chapter.

Additionally, the more times a price bounces off a trendline, the more established the trendline. However, retroactively, as soon as a trendline can be drawn, even if it only encompasses two highs or two lows, should be drawn, as later, the price may come to test the same trendline and you can sooner use it to guide trading decisions.

So, you have seen bullish bearish and horizontal patterns firsthand and even drawn some yourself, but why stop there? Have a go at drawing some trend lines yourself on a range of stocks!

It is also worth saying that no matter how perfectly a chart fits the trendlines, this will never be 100% perfect. Market conditions could change at any point, especially if there is a lot of news affecting markets or company news. This could adversely affect the price of your stock despite the technicals looking good until that point.

If you have money in an airline stock and a breaking news reported on a plane crash from that company, the stock is going to drastically change.

Trendlines will let us make better informed trading decisions, but with a certain margin or error.

So now you understand what trendlines are and how to apply them onto a trading chart, we can start to discover the different types of patterns we will see.

Candlestick Patterns

Over time, price movements form an arrangement of usually 2 or 3 candlesticks based on market behavior that can hint at the possible future direction of the price movement. As such, in each case, the completion of the pattern formation can be a buy or sell signal for traders.

There are lots of candlestick patterns and thankfully, most trading charts come with the ability to automatically plot these, so you do not have to remember each one. They are not a standalone buy or sell signal, instead should be used alongside other indicators to add conviction to your trades or add evidence to determining the trend. The effect of most of these candlestick patterns occurs over the next several periods, and so are more significant when discovered on the higher timeframes.

Some of the most popular patterns include:

- **Bullish Engulfing & Bearish Engulfing**

Bullish engulfing is a candlestick pattern of at least one bearish candle followed by a bullish candle that "engulfs" the bearish candle – the bullish candle engulfs when the body is larger than the preceding bearish candle. This indicates that buyers are taking over sellers in the market and that the price could continue higher.

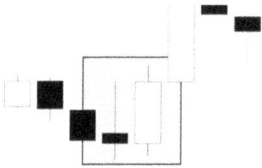

Similarly, a bearish engulfing is where a bearish candle engulfs a smaller bullish candle, meaning sellers are taking over buyers in the market, and that the price could continue to decline further.

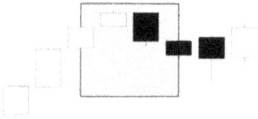

- **Morning Star & Evening Star**

An evening star is a rare but quite reliable bearish pattern that suggests that a bullish trend may soon reverse. It is characterized by a bullish candle followed by a small bullish candle or doji, then by a bearish candle that closes somewhere near the middle of the first candle, a sign that sellers are taking over price action, and that further selling could continue.

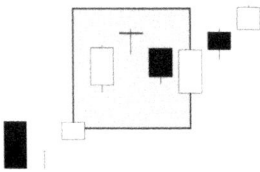

A morning star is the opposite of the evening star and is a bullish pattern in a bearish trend.

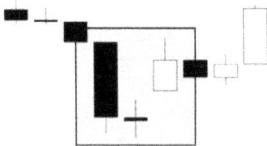

A bearish/bullish abandoned baby is like the morning and evening star and consists of three candles, the first a large bearish/bullish candle and the second candle being a doji that gaps below/above the first candle. The third candle then gaps above/below the doji. This makes an abandoned baby extremely rare and quite an accurate reversal pattern when seen.

- **Bearish & Bullish Harami**

A bearish harami is when a small bearish candle appears completely contained within the body of the last candle, which should be a bullish candle. These should appear in a bullish trend and can signal that a trend reversal is coming.

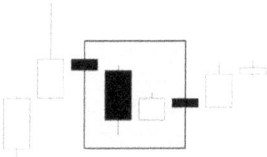

A bullish harami is the opposite and is a bullish pattern in a bearish trend.

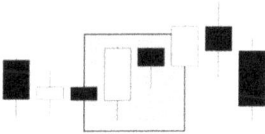

A harami cross is the rarer version of harami in which the second candle is a doji. The interpretation is the same.

- **Falling & Rising Three Methods**

The falling three methods is a five-candlestick pattern that includes a large bearish candle, followed by three, smaller bullish candles that all lie between the first candle's opening and closing price. The final fifth candle is another large bearish candle that closes below the closing prices of the previous four candles. The indication is that buyers in the market momentarily gained control of the price but there are enough sellers and the bearish trend is likely to continue.

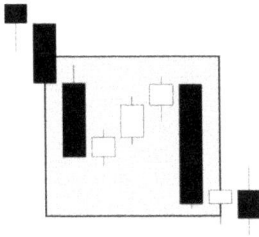

The rising three methods is the opposite. One large bullish candle, followed by three bearish candles and a final large bullish candle indicates that the bullish trend may continue.

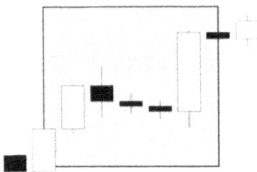

These are some of the most commonly occurring candlestick patterns, but there are plenty more out there, some of which can be automatically added onto the trading chart. In each case, the patterns are only valid after they are completed, and one should use caution when trying to retroactively trade on developing patterns before they are confirmed.

Candlestick patterns are one type of pattern that can recur on the trading chart, the other important type are price patterns.

Price Patterns

Price patterns are recognizable patterns formed by the price movement of an asset. These price patterns form the staple to technical analysis theory, since price history tends to repeat itself, and thus identifying them as they happen can tell us where the trend is likely to go, offer us good buy and sell signals and even tell us an expected price target.

Initially, spotting these patterns may be tricky – and its only made harder by the fact that some patterns are like each other. As with many things - practice makes perfect; the best thing you can do is retrospectively look at the patterns on stocks and assets you are interested in investing into. Note that these patterns are also never 100% perfect.

Consolidation

We have already covered bullish and bearish price movement and touched on horizontal price movement, known as consolidation.

Consolidation is horizontal price movement that bounces within a channel of support and resistance. Consolidation generally occurs from indecision of the buyers and sellers, and can last for a few days, or a few months, or anywhere in between. Consolidation is an important pattern to establish and when you see one, it is good to keep an eye on it as large price movements can follow.

Fig. 26: *Macy's (M) D1 2021 (Mar-Sep) with volume added and trendlines annotated.*

In Fig. 26, MACY's price action can be seen moving horizontally between a channel, the price testing both support and resistance several times before breaking out. A telltale sign of a consolidation period is that the volume (indicated by the bars at the bottom of the chart) is typically lower than when the stock is trending up or down. We can especially see this here when we compare the average volume within the channel and the volume upon the breakout in mid-August. This increase in volume when the prices break through the resistance is a good sign that the breakout from this consolidation – or any chart pattern for that matter - is substantiated. We will look at the price and volume relationship in more detail in the Volume section of the technical indicators chapter.

Additionally, if you are buying this stock for the long term and the current market is in consolidation; you can get that same stock for a discount when you are buying close to the established support level.

Consolidation does not just occur in a channel where support and resistance are parallel – trendlines can vary in their directions, and several different types of consolidation patterns can occur, each hinting at a particular outcome.

Triangles

Triangles are continuation patterns that typically suggest that the price will continue its current trend. They form when consolidation occurs in a trend, and what results at the end is often a large price movement. The most common 3 are the ascending triangle, the descending triangle, and the symmetrical triangle. In each case, the price consolidates within a channel of two trendlines that get narrower as the price consolidates. The trading volume usually decreases as the triangles get narrower, and a breakout of these trendlines are met with an increase in volume.

A symmetrical triangle is a pattern that has two trendlines, one forming a bearish line of resistance, and the other forming a bullish line of support. They are roughly symmetrical in the sense that if either line were flipped horizontally, the steepness of the lines would match. The symmetrical triangle is a continuation pattern, its implication suggesting that a large price movement will occur. This price movement is either breaking out in a bullish direction or falling below into a bearish direction, and the symmetrical triangle gives no indication for one or the other.

Fig. 27: *Amazon Inc. (AMZN) D1 2019-2020 (Aug-Feb)*

The symmetrical triangle, as shown in Fig. 27, provides a signal to buy or sell when the price breaks through either support or resistance, and in this case, we would buy upon the price breakout through the resistance at around $90. If we managed to spot this triangle and bought, we may have ridden the price up from $90 to $108 at its peak, a profit of 20%.

An ascending triangle features two trendlines, a roughly horizontal line of resistance and a bullish line of support. The price movement trades (consolidates) within the ascending triangle, testing the line of support at least twice and trading in a narrower price range, before breaking out on the upside and continuing the bullish trend.

In Fig. 28, the price tested the line of resistance on 7 separate days before breaking out and continuing the upwards movement.

Fig. 28: *Walgreens Boots Alliance Group Inc. (WBA) D1 2000 (March-July) with an ascending triangle annotated.*

A descending triangle features two trendlines, a roughly horizontal line of support and a bearish line of resistance. The price movement trades (consolidates) within the descending triangle, testing the line of support at least twice and trading in a narrower price range, before breaking out on the upside and continuing the bullish trend.

In Fig. 29, the price tested the line of support on 3 separate days before breaking out and continuing the upwards movement.

Fig. 29: *NIO Inc. (NIO) D1 2021 – 2022 (Oct-Feb) with descending triangle annotated.*

In each case, the pattern also gives us a price target once a breakout is confirmed. The price target is where we expect the price to reach and is determined by taking the difference (height) between the resistance and the support at the earliest point of the triangle, and then adding or subtracting it from the price at which the breakout occurred.

In Fig. 30, AMZN tested resistance at $92.84 then dropped to support at $84.18, representing a difference of $8.60. This same difference is applied to the price target when AMZN breaks through resistance at $90.85, where the price target becomes $90.85 + $8.60 which is $99.33. Once the price target is reached, it may form a good place to take profits. Conversely, if in our example AMZN fell below the support level at the same point in time instead of breaking through resistance, we can set a price target of $87.26 (the support at the current time) - $8.60, which is $78.66.

Fig. 30: *Amazon Inc. (AMZN) D1 2019-2020 (Aug-Feb) with volume applied and price targets annotated for a symmetrical triangle.*

The calculation for price targets in ascending and descending triangles is the same. In the case of the ascending triangle in WBA, the earliest test of resistance is around $30, and the earliest test of support is $25, giving a difference of $5. This means that upon breakout through the $30 resistance, the price target becomes $30 + $5 which is $35 – a 17% profit if attained. With the descending triangle in NIO, the earliest resistance is $43, the support is $28, so by the same calculation, the price target upon falling through the support level is $13 – a 107% profit short sell if attained.

Finally, notice the volume indicator at the bottom of the triangle. When any triangle forms, the price consolidates in the triangle, meaning that volume should generally decrease during the length of the triangle. It doesn't need to be a constant decline throughout, but if the volume is consistently increasing in the triangle, it is not as likely to succeed. The volume should also increase when the price breaks out of the triangle. This indicates that there is momentum, meaning the price is much more likely to hit the price target.

Wedges

Wedges are similar in features to triangles – both feature converging trendlines, have the same calculation for price target, decreasing trading volume followed by an increase once a breakout occurs, but the difference are that both trendlines are angled in a bullish or bearish direction, and their indication of a reversal instead of a continuation. When angled bullish, this is a rising wedge, and when angled bearish, this is a falling wedge. Both types are good indicators for a possible trend reversal.

A rising wedge, shown in Fig. 31, shows an initial downtrend, followed by temporary bullish price movement. The price of TSLA hits $270 and bounces back to a higher price than last time. The price falls to a higher low at around $285 on the support then bounces back to an even higher high at resistance. In Fig. 32, the price action trading in the wedge is shown to be accompanied by decreasing volume, until the price falls below the support level and continuing the downtrend prior to the wedge formation. The breakout of the price from the wedge is usually accompanied by increasing volume, suggesting the price action is substantiated.

Fig. 31: *Tesla Inc. (TSLA) H4 2022 (Apr-May) with the rising wedge annotated.*

The price target here for TSLA, shown in Fig. 32, would be the breakout price minus the difference in the earliest tests of the support and resistance which is roughly $30. The price target is therefore around the $270 mark since breakout below support occurred at $300.

Fig. 32: *Tesla Inc. (TSLA) H4 2022 (Apr-May) with the volume applied and rising wedge and corresponding price targets annotated.*

In Fig. 33, we see another example of a rising wedge and the subsequent price target on Bitcoin. Notice the gradual rise, followed by a sharp decline upon the breakout below the support – a typical feature of rising wedges.

Fig. 33: *BTC/USDT D1 2022 (Jun-Sept) with the rising wedge and price target annotated.*

The rising wedge can be inverted to give opposite signals such as that in a falling wedge.

The falling wedge has the same characteristics, but opposite implications compared to the rising wedge. The price bounces between a support and resistance level that are both pointing downwards, and volume decreases when price is trading inside the wedge. We see this in Fig. 34, as well as price break through the resistance on an increase in volume and continuing upwards to meet a 24% price target before sharply retracing.

Fig. 34: *Nvidia Inc. (NVDA) D1 2021-2022 (Dec-Apr) with the volume added and the falling wedge and price target annotated.*

To recollect – wedges always have both trendlines in the same direction.

Flags & Pennants

The flag price pattern is a popular and widely used continuation pattern in technical analysis. It is formed when a security experiences a large, high-volume price movement, followed by a brief consolidation period before continuing its original trend. The flag pattern is often seen as a pause or a period of consolidation before the next leg of the trend resumes. The pattern resembles a flag on a flagpole, with the flagpole representing the initial price movement and the flag itself representing the consolidation.

A bullish flag occurs during an uptrend and is characterized by a sharp upward price movement (the flagpole), followed by a downward-sloping consolidation (the flag) that forms as the price retraces some of its earlier gains. The flag is typically composed of parallel trendlines, creating a rectangular or slightly downward-sloping channel. A breakout above the upper trendline of the flag indicates that the uptrend is likely to continue, and traders may enter long positions or add to their existing long positions.

In Fig. 35, the DXY has been in a strong uptrend for several months and temporarily pauses in October. The pullback is modest, and a price channel can be seen forming, forming the "flag" section of the bull flag. Upon breakout out of the flag, the bullish trend resumes, and the price target is set as same distance as the flagpole entering the flag.

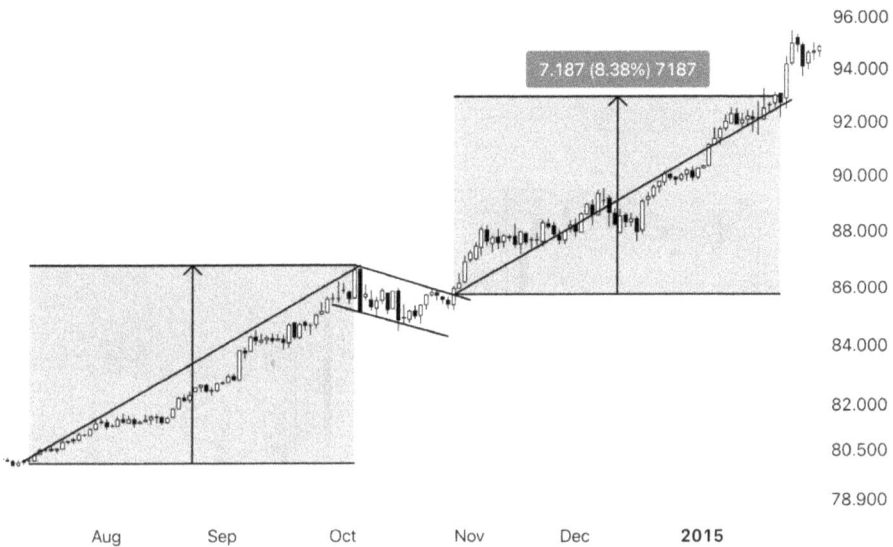

Fig. 35: *U.S. Dollar Strength Index (DXY) D1 2014-2015 (Jul-Jan) with bull flag annotations and expected price target.*

A bearish flag occurs during a downtrend and is characterized by a sharp downward price movement (the flagpole), followed by an upward-sloping consolidation (the flag) that forms as the price retraces some of its earlier losses. Like the bullish flag, the flag is typically made from parallel trendlines, creating a rectangular or slightly upward-sloping channel. The volume in this channel should be decreasing. A breakout below the lower trendline of the flag indicates that the downtrend is likely to continue, and traders may enter short positions.

In Fig. 36, we see a sharp decline in price on large volume, forming the flagpole. We then see price consolidate in an upwards sloping channel on decreasing volume, forming the flag. Finally, when the price breaks below support, a short can be opened, with the price target being the length of the initial flagpole, in this case, a 14% trade.

Fig. 36: *Enphase Energy (ENPH) H4 2022 (Aug-Oct) with bear flag annotations and expected price target.*

The price targets for both bull and bear flags are based on the height of the flagpole going into the flag, projecting the same distance from the breakout point. For example, if the flagpole is 10 points high and the breakout occurs at 50, the price target for a bullish flag would be 60 (50 + 10), while the target for a bearish flag would be 40 (50 - 10).

A pennant looks like a symmetrical flag but behaves like a flag. It is formed after a strong trending move and is interpreted as a brief consolidation before the trend resumes.

In Fig. 37, BTC/USDT exhibits a strong downwards move in May, forming the flagpole. Like the flag, the flagpole height is used as the price target upon a breakout from the pennant. The price consolidates briefly until the pennant is broken to the downside. The trendline break is met with strongly bearish price action and the 32% price target is met in just under a week.

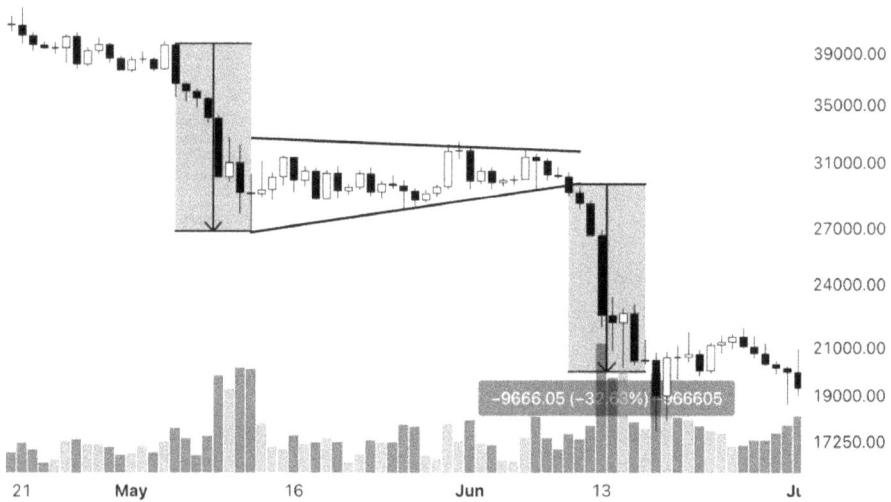

Fig. 37: *BTC/USDT D1 2022 (Apr-Jun) with volume applied and the trendlines and price targets annotated.*

So far, we have looked at patterns that indicate a trend will continue. The following patterns are ones that occur in trend reversals. Trend reversal patterns should display divergences in price and volume, as recall that the volume increases in the direction of the trend. Therefore, if a trend reversal pattern occurs in a previous bullish trend, we would want to look for increases in volume upon corrections and decreases in volume upon rallies.

Double Tops & Double Bottoms

Double tops and double bottoms are a trend reversal pattern where a price rises or falls to a similar level on 2 separate occasions respectively. The archetypal double top looks like an M, and the double bottom a W, and both are signs of a trend reversal. In the double top, the price is usually trending upwards, where it reaches a local peak and retraces down to a neckline level. The price trends upwards again to hit a similar price to the previous peak and retraces down to the neckline again. This time, the price breaks below the neckline and starts on a bearish trend. The double bottom is the double top in reverse, where the trend is reversed from bearish to bullish.

These patterns are more complex in nature, sometimes looking distorted or a mix between a double top/bottom and a head and shoulders pattern yet being totally valid. Other times, it can end up being a different chart pattern – as you will see in trading a breakout chapter - so using them in conjunction with other indicators is desirable.

In Fig. 38, a double top pattern forms after an extended uptrend and indicates a potential bearish reversal. It occurs when the price reaches a significant resistance level, retraces to a support level called the neckline, and then retests the same resistance level without breaking through it. The inability of the price to breach the resistance level for a second time suggests that the bullish momentum is waning and that a downtrend may follow. A great way to confirm the implication of the double top and double bottom (and any other chart pattern) is to observe the price-volume relationship when price appears to be forming a suspected double top or double bottom. Ideally, the price and volume is displaying a divergence, and the break down below the neckline, circled in Fig. 39 should be accompanied by an increase in volume and large bearish candles, indicating bearish momentum.

Fig. 38: *Netflix Inc. (NFLX) D1 2018 (Aug-Oct) with the volume added and double top annotations.*

The double top is confirmed when the price breaks below the neckline, where the price target is achieved by subtracting the difference from the double top resistance and neckline from the price level of the neckline. This makes the price target around $600, after calculating $640 – ($680 – $640) as visualized in Fig. 39.

Fig. 39: *Netflix Inc. (NFLX) D1 2018 (Aug-Oct) with the volume applied, double top annotations and the corresponding price target, and price-volume relations annotated.*

Opposite of the double top pattern, the double bottom pattern forms after an extended downtrend and indicates a potential bullish reversal.

Fig. 40: *S&P 500 Index (SPX) D1 from 2015 – 2016 (Dec-Apr) with the double bottom annotations.*

It occurs when the price reaches a significant support level, retraces to a neckline, and then retests the same support level without breaking through it. The inability of the price to breach the support level for a second time suggests that the bearish momentum is waning and that an uptrend may follow. The trend reversal is confirmed when the price breaks through the neckline. The SPX achieves this, triggering a buy signal with a price target at 2090pts – calculated in the same way as a double top.

Triple Tops & Triple Bottoms

A triple bottom and a triple top are identical in implication to a double bottom and double top respectively. The triple top / bottom tests a resistance or support three times, meaning that it should make the breakout from the neckline even more forceful when it occurs.

Fig. 41: *Gold D1 2022 – 2023 (Jun-Jan) with the triple bottom annotations. A retest is circled.*

Head & Shoulders

The head and shoulders pattern, like the double tops and bottoms are a trend reversal pattern. When the price is trending either bullish or bearish and forms a head and shoulders pattern, once the pattern completes, the price action thereafter should be the opposite trend.

The price creates a small peak that drops to a neckline, where a second larger peak forms the head and the local high point. The price returns to the neckline and a third smaller peak form before returning to the neckline. The price breaking past the neckline after the right signal forms a buy or sell signal. The price target upon a breakout of a head and shoulders pattern is the distance between the head peak and the neckline.

Fig. 42: *McDonalds Inc. (MCD) D1 2021–2022 (Oct-Mar) with the head and shoulders pattern annotated, the neckline shown by the dotted line, and the breakout circled.*

In Fig. 42, MCD in the beginning follows an uptrend going into the head and shoulders pattern. The price after completing the head retraces down to a similar level to the previous retracement. The uptrend is showing weakness here, with the right shoulder unable to form a new high. The pattern is confirmed when the price breaks below the neckline at $246 (circled) where a trader may place a sell order. The price target from this pattern is $222, a 9.7% trade. In this instance, MCD, initially slow, does continue its downtrend to form a successful trade.

Additionally, when we see a head and shoulders pattern forming, we want to see a decrease in trading volume when prices go up, and an increase in volume when prices go down.

Fig. 43: *The same MCD chart from fig. 1 with the volume indicator applied and price-volume divergences annotated.*

In Fig. 43, we see that almost all throughout the head and shoulders pattern, the price and volume did the opposite of each other. When price increased, volume decreased and vice versa.

This is a bearish sign, indicating technical weakness in the bullish trend and confirming the possibility of a trend reversal soon.

Head and shoulders patterns can also be inverted to give a trend reversal pattern with the opposite implication.

Fig. 44: *Apple Inc. (AAPL) H4 2018-2019 (Nov-Feb) with the inverse head & shoulders and corresponding price targets annotated.*

In Fig. 44, AAPL begins with a bearish trend heading into 2019. There are some sharp selloffs that form the left shoulder and head of the inverse head and shoulders pattern. The price gradually rises, before a pullback forms the right shoulder and a defined neckline. Watching the neckline, we see a definitive breakout as a breakaway gap and the price target, the distance between the low and the neckline, is met in due course.

Cup & Handle

The cup and handle is a pattern that presents itself quite literally. The cup refers to a U-shaped dip, followed by a sideways to down trending handle, that results in a bullish trend. It is a bullish continuation pattern that signals a potential reversal of a downtrend or a consolidation in an uptrend, followed by a breakout and continuation of the prevailing uptrend. The pattern resembles a teacup with a handle and typically forms over an extended period, ranging from a few weeks to several months.

The cup forms when an asset experiences a rounded bottom after a downtrend or a consolidation period. The cup should have a U-shape with relatively equal highs on both sides, indicating that the stock has found a bottom and is starting to recover. The depth of the cup should not be overly steep or V-shaped, as a smoother, more gradual recovery is preferred.

The handle forms after the completion of the cup and is characterized by a smaller, downward-sloping consolidation period. The handle typically takes the shape of a bull flag or a pennant and should not retrace more than 50% of the cup's advance. The handle formation can last anywhere from a few days to several weeks, and its volume should be lower than the volume during the formation of the cup, indicating a pause in the uptrend.

The cup and handles price targets are based on the depth of the cup, projecting the same distance from the breakout point. For example, if the cup's depth is 10 points and the breakout occurs at 50, the price target would be 60 (50 + 10).

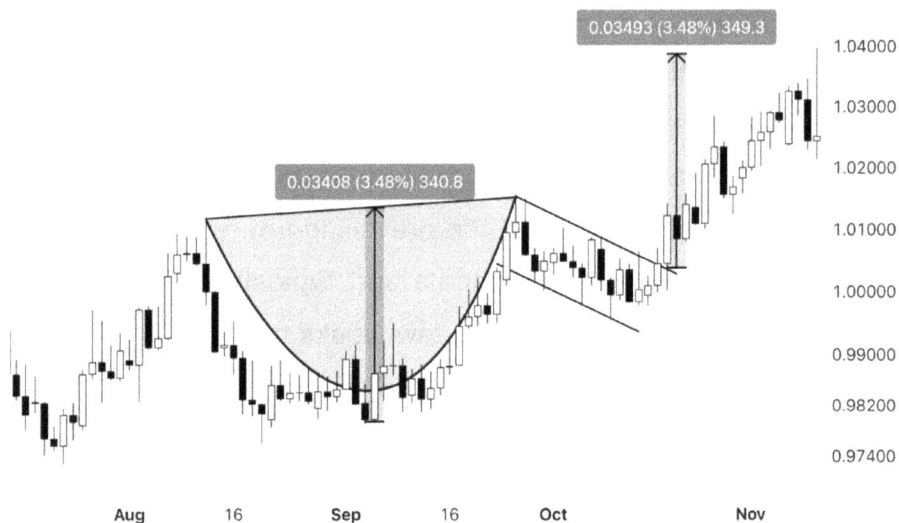

Fig. 45: *AUD/CAD D1 2016 (Jul-Nov) with the cup & handle pattern and corresponding price targets annotated.*

In Fig. 45, the AUD/CAD currency pair rises to around parity at 1.00 before pulling back to a low of 0.98. We measure the low of the cup to the resistance connecting the two sides of the cup to give us the distance of our price target. Following the formation of our cup, we look for a bull flag or pennant within the following price action and monitor for any breakouts.

Gaps

Gaps are a common price pattern, typically represented on a candlestick or bar chart. A gap occurs when there is a significant difference between the closing price of one trading period and the opening price of the following trading period, with no trading activity occurring in the price range between these two points.

Gaps are generally the result of important news, events, or announcements affecting the market or a specific security, causing a sudden shift in sentiment or trading activity. There are four primary types of gaps:

- **Common Gaps** - Common gaps occur as a part of normal trading activity and typically do not have any significant implications for the future price direction. They can be caused by various factors, such as lower liquidity, overnight price fluctuations, or minor news events. Common gaps are usually small and tend to be filled relatively quickly, meaning that the price eventually returns to the level at which the gap occurred.

- **Breakaway Gaps** - Breakaway gaps are considered more significant as they occur at the beginning of a new trend or after the completion of a significant chart pattern. This type of gap usually forms on high trading volume and is accompanied by a significant change in market sentiment. Breakaway gaps are considered a strong signal for trend continuation and are less likely to be filled in the short term.

- **Runaway Gaps** - Runaway gaps, also known as continuation or measuring gaps, occur during an ongoing trend and signal that the current trend is likely to continue. These gaps are often seen as a confirmation of the prevailing trend and are typically accompanied by high trading volume. Like breakaway gaps, runaway gaps are less likely to be filled in the short term.

- **Exhaustion Gaps** - Exhaustion gaps occur at the end of a strong trend and signal that the trend is about to reverse. These gaps form when the market participants make a final push in the direction of the prevailing trend, but the momentum is not sustained, leading to a harsh reversal. Exhaustion gaps are usually accompanied by high trading volume and are more likely to be filled, as the market reverts to its previous price levels.

Fig. 46: *Bank of America Corp. (BAC) D1 2021-2022 (Nov-Feb) with volume applied and an exhaustion gap annotated.*

Gaps can also be used to form a resistance or take profit level on the trading chart. A common occurrence when gaps are formed is for subsequent price movement to close the gap.

This strategy is known as playing the gap and can work particularly well, especially if the gap formed is a contra trend gap. For example, if the trend is bearish, but a gap formed pushes prices higher, the chances that the gap is closed soon are greatly increased.

Fig. 47: *SPDR Dow Jones Industrial Average ETF (DIA) M15 2022 (Dec) with volume applied and target based on gap annotated.*

In Fig. 47, the DIA in the first half of December 2022 has been in an uptrend, but has shown signs of a trend reversal, indicators that we will discuss later have given us a signal several days prior from this gap of a trend reversal. The DIA nonetheless gaps higher on the opening day, but within the first two or three candles, we can see that the upwards momentum in unsustainable and within the same trading day, the gap is closed.

When not immediately filled, gaps can also be used to form a resistance or take profit level over a longer timeframe on the trading chart.

Fig. 48: *Dow Jones Industrial Average (DJI) D1 2022 (May-Aug). The DJI creates two gaps in June 2022, which are "closed" at times where price intersects the dotted target line, circled on the chart.*

Here in Fig. 48, two runaway gaps form throughout June, continuing the bearish trend that has been in play up until that point. The DJI begins to recover and closes the first gap before a pullback occurs. The DJI then rallies at the start of July, only to find resistance at the level the gap was opened at.
Eventually, the price breaks through the resistance and tests

the second gap as a resistance, before a small retracement and a subsequent closing the gap at the start of August.

Trading A Breakout

A breakout is a move above a resistance trendline or below a support trendline, accompanied by an increase in volume and volatility, as other traders trade on the breakout. A breakout above a resistance should imply a long position, and a breakout below support should imply a short position.
Once you have identified a price pattern breakout, you should establish a position upon reasonable confirmation.

This confirmation should include:
- Large candles upon breakout
- Large volatility, particularly visible on low timeframes
- Increase in volume

A convincing breakout will look something like the one circled in Fig. 49. Here, the Japanese Market Index NIKKEI breaks down from a triangle price pattern. In hindsight it is easy to see, but retroactively at the time, we look for confirmation of this breakdown using our checklist above. The breakdown has indeed been accompanied by a large bearish candle, much larger than preceding candles, and we do see an increase in volume. On lower timeframes (not shown) such as the 5-minute or 15-minute chart, we would also expect to see larger candles, than previous candles, indicating volatility is increasing.

Fig. 49: *Nikkei 225 (NIKKEI) D1 2016-2017 (Nov-May) with the volume applied and trendlines annotated.*

Once you have established a position, you should set a stop loss and take profit for the trade. The take profit should be positioned at the price target that is calculated for the price pattern in question.

The stop loss should be set close to the trendline where the breakout occurred. If you have a long position, then it should be set slightly below the resistance. For a short position, it should be set slightly above the support. How close the stop loss should be set is down to your taste for risk – a good rule of thumb is that the risk to reward (R/R) ratio should sit at 3 or above. So, if your first take profit is at 3% above the trendline, the stop should be no one than 1% below. The stop loss should not be too close to the trendline either, as the markets operate within a margin of error and the trendlines you have drawn are rarely perfect. Think of this margin of error as other traders drawing the same trendlines slightly differently and using them to guide their trading activity.

Often, when trading the breakout, you will see the price pullback to the trendline where the breakout occurred (a retest). The critical point here is to watch for the price to bounce off. The trendline where the breakout occurred should swap roles, so a resistance breakout should now act as a support and vice versa. If the trendline fails here, then it is typically a failed breakout although the price may be still within a margin of error.

Using the same example of NIKKEI in Fig. 50, we see a triangle pattern with several tests on both support and resistance. We have had the charts drawn up and have been watching developments within the price movement – and finally, we see a breakdown from the triangle below the support, as confirmed previously.

The price target is determined to be a 5% trade, but accounting for the confirmation we were waiting for earlier, we enter the trade slightly below the trendline, and the trade becomes a 4.72% one. The stop loss is placed a little above the bottom of the triangle, which should now be a resistance.

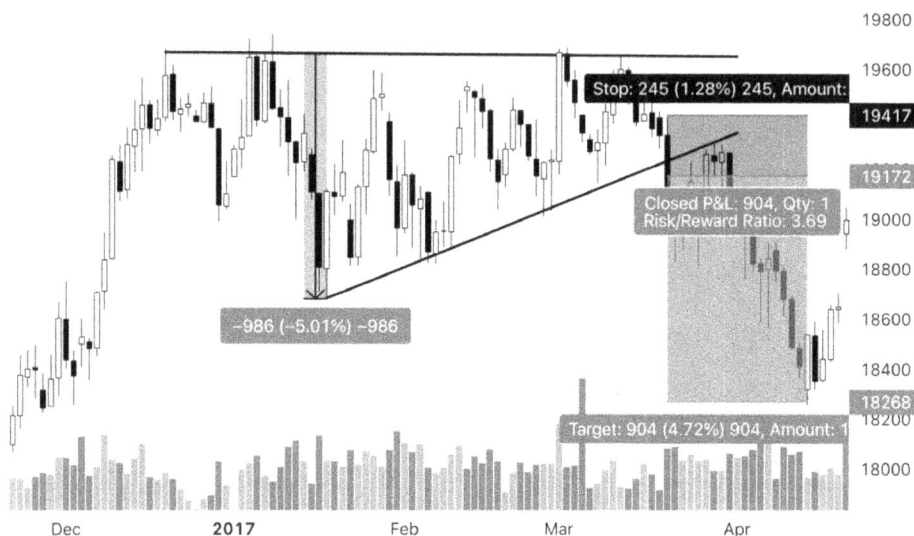

Fig. 50: *Nikkei 225 (NIKKEI) D1 2016-2017 (Nov-May) with the volume applied and short position annotated with target, stop and R/R.*

Since the trade is 4.72%, we are happy to give the stop loss a little room and position it at the last candle's high before the breakout, making the stop loss a 1.28% loss and giving a nice risk to reward (R/R) of 3.69. Gauging the R/R is important when setting the stop loss, as if the R/R is too low, then the statistical failure of price patterns will wipe out gains over time. As price breaks down, notice how it goes to retest the triangle support as a resistance at a higher point, and so such a tight stop loss by the point of entry into a short would have been stopped out. The price goes on after the retest to reach the take profit level. On this occasion, the R/R is 3.69 but if we caught the price right on the trendline, the R/R would have improved to 5. The more you wait for the price to leave the breakout, the lower the R/R, so trading the breakout is a balance between waiting for confirmation and maximizing R/R. If the R/R slips too low before confirmation, then you should not enter the trade.

Sometimes, breakouts will fail – these are known as fakeouts, or more formally, whipsaws. Whilst sometimes these will occur despite everything forecast to work, in other cases, fakeouts come with some advance warning signs.

Fig. 51: *Zoom Inc. (ZM) H4 2020 (Jun-Aug) with the volume applied and "double top" pattern, divergences and the fakeout annotated.*

In Fig. 51, ZM has been in a bullish trend for several months and heading into July, it appears that volume is declining as prices are rising, a bearish divergence between price and volume hints at a potential reversal. The price makes a high in mid-July, then pulls back to a support level before making a lower high at the start of August on low volume. There have been three warning signs now of a potential trend reversal. We also now have a potential double top pattern, with an established neckline, giving us the fourth reason, we could see a trend reversal. The price declines in August, and volume modestly increases. During August 11, the prices break below the established neckline, where we open a short and set a price target at roughly $195, a 17% trade, and we set a stop loss at the high of the last candle, at about a 4% loss.

Unfortunately for us, as soon as the breakout occurs, the prices start to head back up and above our neckline, back into the trading range between the neckline and resistance. Furthermore, notice how the volume starts to increase as prices head back up after the fakeout. Thankfully, our stop loss limited our losses to just 4% - but could we have known that this was going to be a fakeout? After all, we had four pieces of evidence suggested a trend reversal...

The two biggest warning signs was the low volume on the prices decline to the fakeout point, and the previous candle, where the wick broke through the trendline, but not the body. Let's discuss them in order:

1. The low volume as the price declined to the fakeout was probably the bigger warning. Although there was a modest increase in volume compared to the volume at the last peak, the volume, since entering the "double top" pattern was on an overall decline. For a breakout, we need to see a substantial increase in volume on price

declines, and a substantial increase in volume on breaking out.

2. The other warning was the previous candle prior to the black breakout candle. This candle actually broke below the neckline first but closed above it. This activity suggests that the bulls were defending this price level and successfully kept it above the neckline. For the bulls to be overturned, we needed to see an increase in bearish momentum and volume, which was not significant enough.

Finally, on the black fakeout candle, the size was not small but not as large as other candles within the pattern, indicating modest bearish momentum. A good rule of thumb is a successful breakout candle should consist of a large candle where the majority of the body is outside the trading range – in this case, below the neckline.

Zooming out on the price chart of ZM in Fig. 52, we can see after the fakeout, the price rose and ended up breaking above the resistance connecting the double top. The pattern was therefore a bull flag all along, not a double-top and the price went on to meet the price target, a whopping 86% trade in the space of a few months. This example is a great lesson on the need to be adaptable as a trader, and to extend your trendlines on the charts.

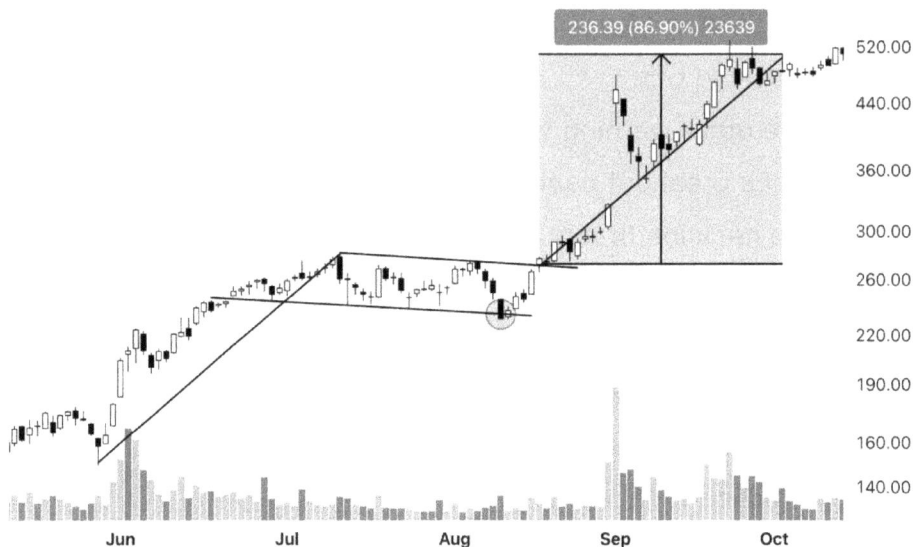

Fig. 52: *Zoom Inc. (ZM) D1 2020 (May-Oct) with the volume applied and bull flag pattern annotated with corresponding price target. The fakeout during the bull flag is circled.*

When looking at the breakout of the bull flag in Fig. 52, although we see the daily candle above the resistance, we don't see the momentum we would ideally like for a breakout, with the breakout candle being smaller than preceding candles in the bull flag indicating weak momentum. These conflicting signs that we are getting reiterates the importance of the weight-of-evidence approach, considering each data as evidence for or against an idea. So far, we have considered trendline breaks, patterns and Dow Theory in our weight-of-evidence approach, but in the next chapter on technical indicators, we will have a wide range of additional data to use as evidence for or against our ideas.

THE TREND
KEY POINTS:

- Trend can be bullish, bearish, or sideways and can occur on any timeframe, from 1-minute to 1-month charts.

- Dow Theory states that bullish trends continue when price is able to make higher highs and higher lows (opposite for bearish trends). Trend reversals are according to peak and trough analysis.

- Consolidation is when price is bound by support and resistance and is accompanied by decreasing volume. They tend to lead to breakouts.

- Trend continuation patterns indicate a continuation of the trend going into the pattern and include wedges, flags and pennants.

- Trend reversal patterns indicate a trend reversal and include double-tops and bottoms and head and shoulders.

- Triangle patterns can result in a trend continuation or a trend reversal.

- A successful breakout is one where price breaks through a trendline with a lot of momentum (large candlesticks) and a lot of volume.

V. Technical Indicators

Technical indicators are indicators that manipulate the price or volume data of an asset to show us its technicals.

These indicators are either superimposed on top of the trading chart (overlays) or separated underneath the trading chart (oscillators).

Indicators, just like price patterns, work on any timeframe, but have greater significance on the longer timeframes. The indicators, just like the technical patterns should be used to add evidence to an analysis of the technical situation, and the more of them pointing to the same conclusion, the greater the conviction we have to that conclusion.

As traders and investors, technical indicators can help by:

- Providing buy and sell signals.
- Confirming price pattern breakouts and trend reversals.
- Analysis of the current trend to spot any weaknesses.

Using Trendlines On Indicators

The same trend determining techniques when it came to constructing trendlines and chart patterns can also be used on the technical indicators discussed. Finding an indicator break through a trendline that it has respected multiple times previous would act as a confirmation when the price breakouts from a price pattern or trendline and should add conviction when trading a breakout.

We will look at examples of how you can construct trendlines and patterns on indicators as we discuss the indicators throughout this chapter.

Volume Indicators

By far the most common volume indicator, or even indicator in general is the trading volume indicator, or just volume. We've covered different applications of volume in patches in earlier sections of this book, but we will assimilate all that information into this more comprehensive section.

Volume

The volume in most settings will be represented by a bar chart that lays at the bottom of a trading chart. The larger the bars in the bar chart, the higher the volume. The default color of the bars is either green (colored light grey here) or red (colored dark grey). When green, over 50% of the volume came from buyers, and red, over 50% of the volume came from sellers.

The value of the trading volume itself in a given period shows us how much liquidity a particular asset has, which is important particularly for smaller and lesser-known investments (such as low liquidity stocks or derivatives offered from a broker) tend to have higher bid-ask spreads (making your trades less profitable). In technical analysis, the main use for the volume indicator concerns its relationship with the price, and its value itself has little use.

The relationship between volume and price can tell us a multitude of information. It can tell us whether a trend is confirmed or unsubstantiated, as we have seen demonstrated in chart patterns and in the Dow Theory. It can also confirm breakouts, where we would expect to see an increase in volume upon a breakout. It can confirm the validity of a particular price pattern, such as a triangle, as consolidation of price within a pattern should come with a general decrease in volume.

In a bullish trend, the trading volume should increase when the price increases, and decrease when the price decreases. In a bearish trend, the trading volume should decrease when the price increases, and increase when the price decreases.
Any deviation to this relationship is known as a **divergence** and hints at a trend reversal.

Summarized in a table:

	Uptrend	Downtrend
Volume ↑ **Price ↑**	- Bullish trend continuation	- Hint at a trend reversal
Volume ↑ **Price ↓**	- Hint at a trend reversal	- Bearish trend continuation
Volume ↓ **Price ↑**	- Hint at a trend reversal	- Bearish trend continuation
Volume ↓ **Price ↓**	- Bullish trend continuation	- Bearish trend continuation (no buyers or sellers) - Hint at a trend reversal when accompanied by volume increase on corrections.

It is important to note that these deviations when they appear are not buy or sell signals, but form part of our analysis along with other indicators as to the technical picture behind an asset. Multiple price-volume divergences in a bullish or bearish trend, should keep a trader on the lookout for any confirmation of a reversal and from other indicators and price patterns.

The reason behind this price - trading volume relationship is that it reflects how other market participants react when price movement occurs in a given trend. If other traders see this as a sustained trend, then they will likely buy into the stock too, pushing up the volume. As the price follows a trend for longer, more traders will buy in. If other traders no longer see the price movement in a trend as sustainable, they will not buy in, and we should see a gradually lowering volume. Upon a correction (price decline), an increase in volume suggests traders are happy to lock in profits, as they no longer view holding the investment to be worth the risk. This increase in sell pressure drives prices down, and without new buyers, prices continue to decline, and a bearish trend has begun.

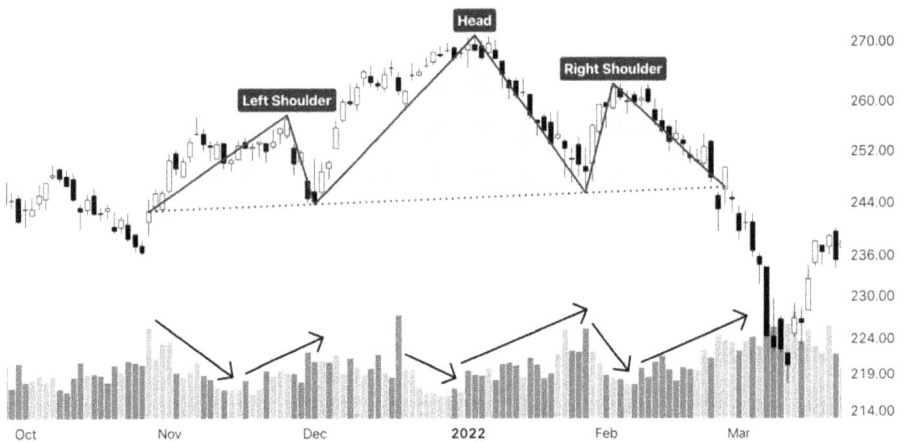

Fig. 53: *McDonalds Inc. (MCD) D1 2021–2022 (Oct-Mar) with the volume applied and head and shoulders pattern, and price-volume relationship annotated.*

The price-volume relationship on MCD demonstrates multiple bearish divergences on the offset of this chart. The trend is bullish as prices push higher, but the volume tells a different story as notice on every advance in price to a higher high is met with declining volume, and every pullback is met with an increase in volume.

Upon completion of the head, divergences continue as price fails to make a higher high on the right shoulder, and the trend reversal is confirmed upon the completion of the head and shoulders pattern. Note how volume continued to increase as prices headed down in March 2022, signifying that the downtrend is likely to continue.

The volume analysis suggested that a trend reversal was likely, coupled with a trend reversal pattern to give traders and investors a confirmation of the downtrend and an expected price target.

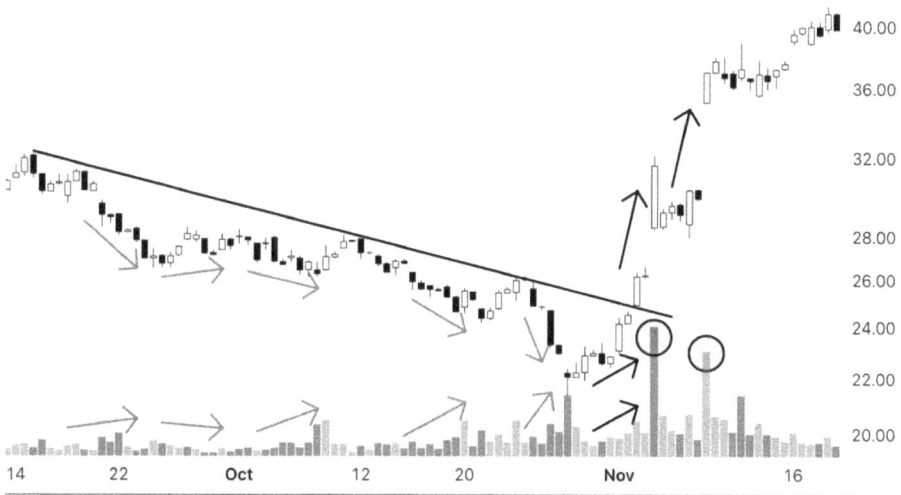

Fig. 54: *Lyft (LYFT) H4 2020 (Sept-Nov) with the volume added and price-volume relationship annotated.*

Looking at LYFT in Fig. 54, we can see a slow and steady decline until the beginning of November 2020. Unlike in MCD previously, we see a normal price-volume relationship in the bearish trend. As the price declines, volume increases and as price rise, volume falls. Furthermore, we have a well-defined bearish trendline. After a selling climax occurs, taking prices down to $22, we see our first hint at brighter times ahead for LYFT. As the price ascends in the beginning of November, so does the volume. In a bearish trend, this is a potential sign of a trend reversal. The prices continue to rise, gapping above our trendline with a large bullish 4-hour candle on rising volume, indicating the bullish momentum is substantiated. We then get two large runaway gaps that occur on huge volume, another confirmation of the new prevailing bullish trend. Upon confirmation on the bullish trend on LYFT after the significant trendline break, it sees it's market price rise from $25 to $40 in the space of 2 weeks, a huge 60% gain! The volume does decrease throughout November, signifying that the bullish trend may be running out of steam.

In Fig. 55, PYPL begins with a bullish trend showing some weakness as volume displays some divergences with price. Nonetheless, the bullish trend continues throughout June and into July, where it begins to form a rising wedge. Since it is a bit unusual to see a rising wedge as a trend-topping pattern, we want to validate its existence using volume. We know that price consolidates within a rising wedge and so we look for declining volume throughout the course of the rising wedge. Indeed, we see a gradual decline in volume as price consolidates in the rising wedge. Finally, around July 20th, we see a breakdown of the rising wedge accompanied by huge volume and a large breakaway gap, the price target of the pattern being met in just a few trading days.

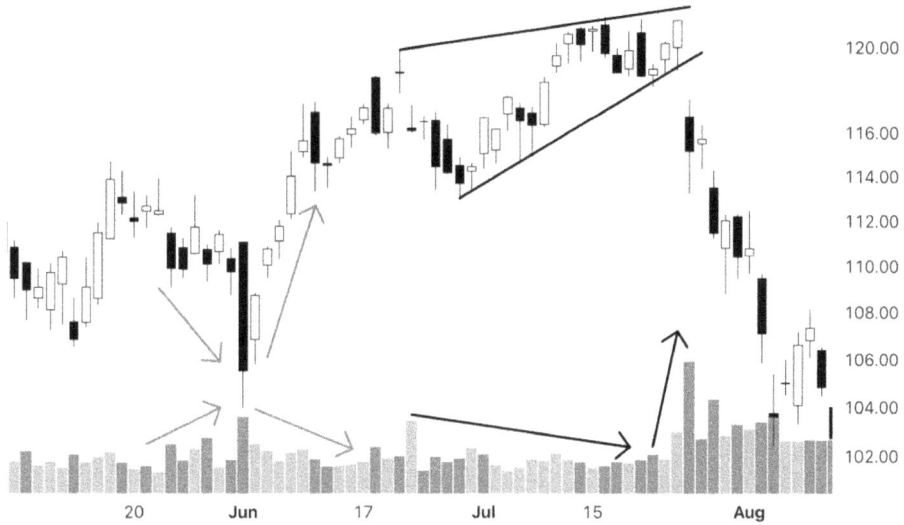

Fig. 55: *PayPal (PYPL) D1 2019 (May-Aug) with the volume applied and the price-volume relationship and rising wedge annotated.*

Fixed Volume Profile Range

The fixed volume profile range (FVPR) is a useful tool in a technician's arsenal. It displays the volume horizontally, showing the trading volume at different price levels over a given timeframe. The FVPR timeframe is selected manually by drawing the indicator over the desired timeframe. The FVPR can be used on any timeframe and should be drawn from a trend low to a trend high or vice versa.

The FVPR shows investors the liquidity at different price levels of a given stock. The significance is, when prices are falling, there will be good buyer support (high liquidity) at price levels with large volume (shown with large bars on the FVPR), and the same price levels should act as a resistance when prices are rising. On the contrary, price levels with low volume can be interpreted as areas without much resistance and support, and hence when price reaches these levels, it is more likely that the price can jump or drop in price until higher volume price levels are met.

The FVPR also displays a horizontal line at the price level where the largest amount of volume has taken place. This is called the price of control (POC), which can be interpreted as a line where bears are in control when price is below, and bulls are in control when price is above.

Fig. 56: *SPDR S&P500 ETF (SPY) D1 2022-2023 (Sept-Jan) with the FVPR added.*

In Fig. 56, the FVPR has been drawn from the Oct 13 low to the Dec 13 high, and we see most of the liquidity occurring at $395, as well as the POC. Bears and bulls fight around the POC during Nov and Dec, almost using it as a resistance and support respectively, before bears decisively take control on Dec 15 & 16. The price plummets, heading down with ease to $380-ish before support is found. Looking at the FVPR, we can see that there was little liquidity between around $385 and $392 and a lot more around $380, explaining the price action we saw in Dec 15 & 16.

What is fascinating about the FVPR on the SPY is that this POC around $395 has been hinted before.

Fig. 57: *SPDR S&P500 ETF (SPY) W1 2020-2022 (Mar-Jan) with the FVPR added.*

Looking at the FVPR from the 2020 low to the 2022 high in Fig. 57, the SPY remarkably gives us a POC of around $390, close to the POC of the previous timeframe, and adding more evidence to the idea that this price around $390-$395 should be a battle zone between bulls and bears.

OBV - On-Balance Volume

The OBV takes the data from the volume one step further and allows a trader to directly compare the price movement to the trading volume movement. This allows traders to see whether price movements are correlated with 'smart money', a term for institutional money rather than retail money. Since most of the volume in the stock market comes from institutional traders and investors, the change is this volume can hint where they are investing.

One of the main ways to utilize OBV within trading is to look for divergences between the OBV line and the price movement of an asset. If the price of a stock is increasing, but the OBV line is flat or decreasing, this could indicate that institutional investors are not buying into the stock or generally selling. The result may be that the price increase may slow and reverse in the future. Conversely, if the price is decreasing, and the OBV is flat or increasing, that could mean that institutional investors are buying in, and therefore the price could begin to increase in the future. If the price is consolidating over the long-term, the OBV could also show whether institutional investors think the price will increase or decrease.

Fig. 58: *Wells Fargo & Company (WFC) D1 2020-2021 (Apr-Jan) with the OBV added.*

With WFC, when connecting the highs, OBV clearly increases with decreasing price (a bullish divergence), suggesting that institutional investors are getting in, and that the stock could increase in price soon. It is not a buy or sell signal, but when confirmed with other indicators, builds up a case to take a long position on WFC.

The OBV can also be used to observe trendline and pattern breakouts and confirm one in the price. Just like on the price, we can draw trendlines on the OBV, and any oscillating indicator for that matter, and look for breakouts from these trendlines and patterns.

In Fig. 59, we can see a double bottom pattern on V with two clear bottoms and a neckline. To further add conviction to a potential trade on this double bottom pattern, we can go to the OBV and what we get is two supporting details from the OBV. First, the OBV also display a double bottom pattern of its own in the same timeframe as the double bottom pattern on the price. Secondly, the lower trendline connecting the bottom is slightly down-trending on price, and up-trending on the OBV, giving us a subtle bullish divergence. When it comes to trading the double bottom pattern, we can make an even higher conviction trade when both the price and the OBV confirms the pattern by breaking out through their respective necklines.

Fig. 59: *Visa Inc. (V) D1 2022 (Jul-Dec) with the OBV added.*

Accumulation/Distribution

Another similar indicator to consider that is interpreted in the same way to OBV is the Accumulation/Distribution. The main difference with the Accumulation/Distribution is that it adds weighting to prices closing near its high as opposed to near the midpoint. The result is that the Accumulation/Distribution line may be interpreted easier in some stocks and assets, so if it is preferred, or if OBV does not work well with the asset you are viewing, give the Accumulation/Distribution a shot. In Fig. 60, the Accumulation/Distribution works well in confirming a bearish trendline break.

Fig. 60: *Apple Inc. (AAPL) H4 2022 (Mar-Aug) with Accumulation/Distribution added.*

Moving Averages

The moving average (MA) is a line graph that shows the average price over a given amount of data points. The average price is the closing price of the stock on a given timeframe. Typically overlayed on the trading chart, the MA can be any amount of data points, a 50-day MA, 200-day, 10-day, 1000-day and so on. The number of data points is correlated to how closely the MA follows the chart. The fewer the number of data points, the quicker the MA will react to changes in the market price.

The MA as an indicator will help us identify buy and sell signals, show us the general trend of the stock, and help us identify stocks that are correlated.

Adding an MA onto a trading chart typically adds a simple moving average (SMA). An SMA is a moving average where data points have the same weight when calculating the MA. The SMA is therefore the default for MA and the terms are used interchangeably.

A single MA on a trading chart can help identify trends. Trends are either bullish, bearish, or sideways, but are sometimes not well recognizable because of short-term volatility. A MA drawn onto the trading chart can easily show a trend. If the MA is moving upwards, it signals a bullish trend, and the MA can act as a level of support. A price drop, close to support, or slightly below the support could indicate a buy signal, as shown in Fig. 61. Here, we see the price of TSLA drop to it's 50-day MA on three separate occasions, highlighted using arrows. On each occasion, a buy upon touching the MA would have yielded a decent trade, particularly on the last arrow.

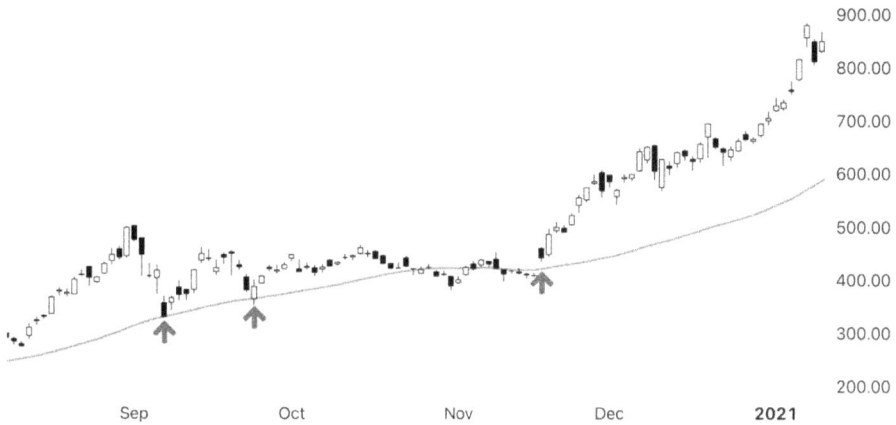

Fig 61: *Tesla Inc. (TSLA) D1 2020-2021 (Aug-Jan) with the 50-day MA plotted.*

A downwards MA is a bearish trend, and the MA could be a line of resistance for the trend. A price moving close to the resistance or slightly above it could be a sell signal, as shown in Fig. 62.

Fig 62: *Tesla Inc. (TSLA) D1 2019 (Jan-Jul) with the 50-day MA plotted.*

Combining two MAs can help us identify a potential trend reversal, as well as buy and sell signals. When the faster MA (less data points, and thus quicker reacting) crosses over the slower MA (more data points, slower reacting), this could indicate a trend reversal in a bullish direction. The popular example takes the 50-day MA as the "fast" MA, and the 200-day MA as the "slow" MA. When the 50-day MA crosses above the 200-day MA, this is known as a golden cross, and is a good buy signal. When the 50-day MA crosses below the 200-day MA, this is known as a death cross, and this could be a sell signal.

Fig 63: *eBay Inc. (EBAY) H4 2020 (May-Oct) with the 50-day and 200-day MAs applied and the death cross and golden cross annotated.*

In Fig. 63, the 50-day MA crosses above the 200-day MA (golden cross) when the price is around $40, and later crosses below the 200-day MA (death cross) again when the price is $52.

Using the MAs in both the ways mentioned above, we can retroactively look at eBay to identify buy and sell opportunities and identify a trend reversal when it occurs.

Looking at Fig. 64, the price begins at $65 and moves in an uptrend, defined by the upwards direction of the MA. Both MAs act as a dynamic line of support in this uptrend, and the price bounces off the 50-day MA (marked by the light grey arrows) and the 200-day MA (marked by the dark grey arrows), signaling some great short-term buy opportunities.

The price begins to decline shortly after the last buy signal, and the death cross where the fast MA crosses over the slow MA can be seen. This confirms a trend reversal from a bullish one to a bearish one, and the 50-day MA switches to become a dynamic line of resistance. The price tests the 50-day MA several times on the way down and each time would have presented a good sell opportunity.

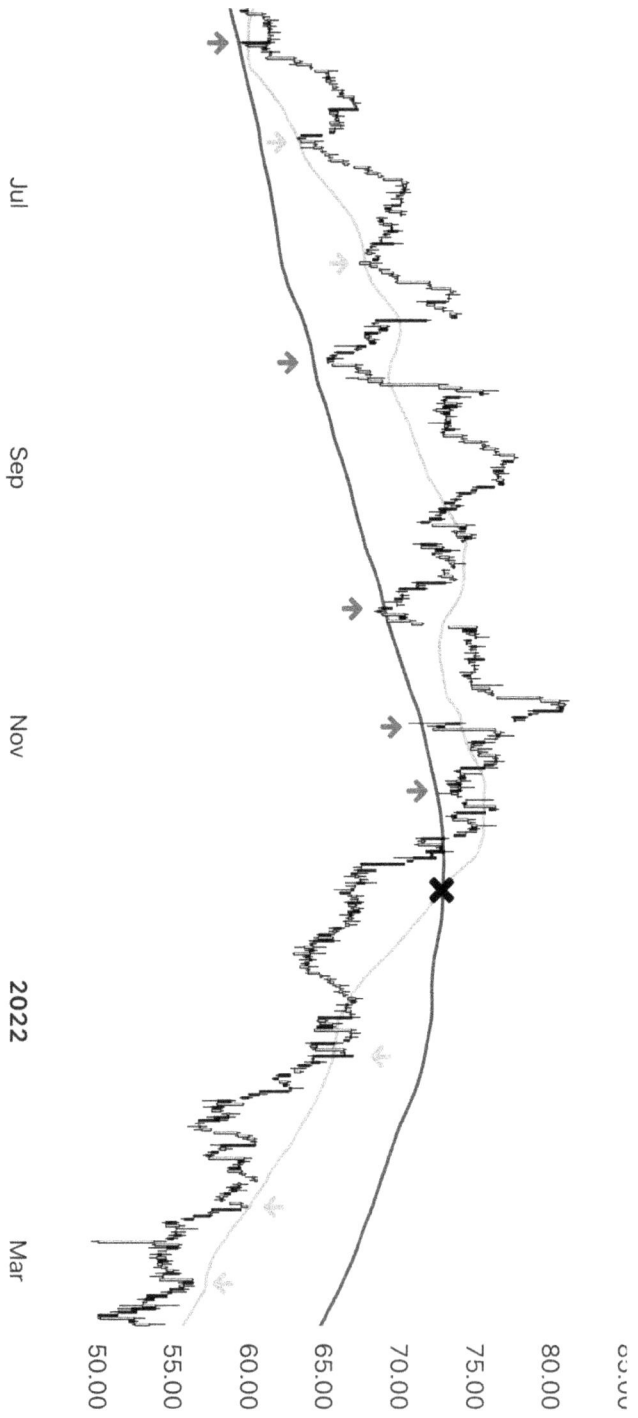

Fig 64: *eBay Inc. (EBAY) H4 2019 (Jan-Jul) with the 50-day MA plotted.*

MAs are typically great for indicating long term trends, as seen with Apple on a multi-year period, but must be used with caution when trends are sharp or changing often.

Fig. 65: *Dow Jones Industrial Average (DJI) D1 2019-2020 with 50-day and 200-day MAs plotted. The golden cross occurs around the 26500pts mark and bullish action follows, until the abrupt 2020 stock market crash. The death cross occurs at the 20000pts mark.*

A great example of MAs weakness is shown in Fig. 65; the Dow here in the lead up to the 2020 stock market crash. A golden cross occurs, and from there the Dow is steadily rising throughout the majority of 2019, but sometime in February of 2020, we can see a drastic change of trend and massive bearish action.

If you took the 50-day MA as the sell signal, you would have sold near the top, the 200-day MA is positioned a little lower – but have a look at the position where the 50- and 200-day MAs cross at the death cross. If you would have sold here, you can see that you would have sold at the bottom of the dip.

This demonstrates that MAs, in particular SMAs, are slow to react to changes in market conditions and does not provide optimal signals when there is rapidly evolving economic news.

The exponential moving average (EMA) rectifies the shortcomings of SMAs by adding weighting proportional to how recent the data point is. The closer the data point to the current date, the more it is taken into account in the MA. The result is a MA that more closely follows the price movement than the corresponding SMA and can therefore detect trend reversals sooner than the SMA. The differences between the SMA and EMA in practice are subtle, and they both produce similar buy and sell signals, but the EMA as demonstrated in Fig. 66 can produce superior signals in quick-changing environments.

Fig. 66: *Dow Jones Industrial Average (DJI) D1 2019-2020 (Aug-Apr) with the 200-day SMA (light grey) and the 200-day EMA (dark grey) plotted. The death crosses of the corresponding 50-day MAs (not shown) have been added.*

Had the 200-day EMA been used over the 200-day SMA, the sell signals would have been sooner, both from the price crossing below the MA and the signal from the death cross.

Both the SMA and EMA are extremely useful in technical analysis, and as such, have been incorporated into several other important technical indicators, one such indicator being the moving average convergence divergence, or MACD for short.

Other moving averages exist, the weighted moving average WMA is another commonly offered MA that can be described as a more extreme example of the EMA.

Momentum Indicators

Momentum is an important concept in technical analysis.
If determining the trend can tell us the direction of the markets, then momentum can tell us the magnitude of which the market is trending. If momentum is declining, then we can reasonably assume that the trend is likely to change in the future.

Momentum indicators reveal to us the strength of the trend in question and can also give us good buy and sell signals. They also introduce to us the concept of **overbought** and **oversold**, which is when momentum is said to be unsustainably bullish or bearish respectively and its interpretation may be that price at least sees some form of correction or pullback in the near future.

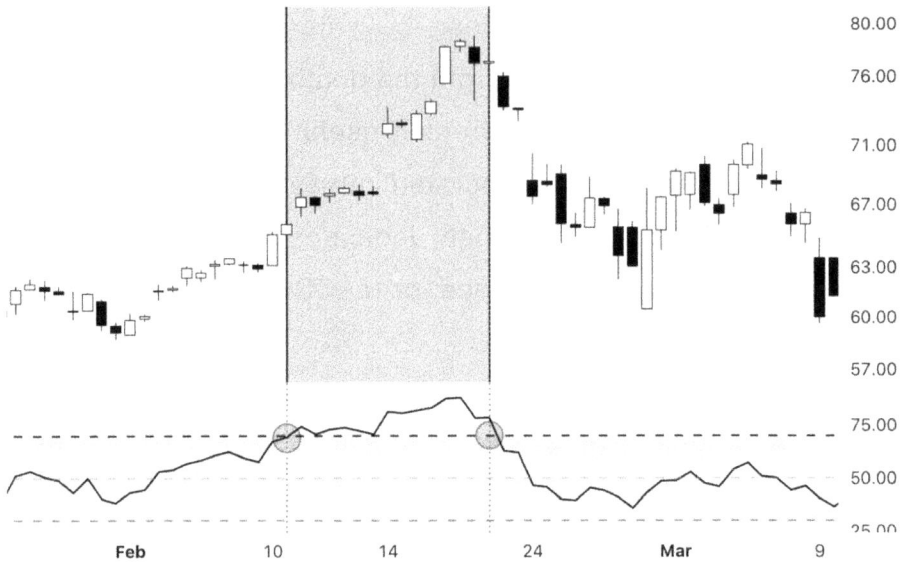

Fig. 67: *Nvidia (NVDA) H4 2020 (Jan-Mar) with the RSI applied, and overbought conditions in price highlighted, with entering and exiting overbought conditions circled.*

In Fig. 67, NVDA becomes overbought on Feb 11 by crossing the upper line on the oscillator (circled), signaling that we might see a correction, or even a reversal in the future. NVDA continues to be overbought and prices push even higher, closing in on $80, when we see prices stumble and no longer overbought on Feb 21. Indeed, the overbought sign foreshadowed an ensuing decline that would wipe almost all gains NVDA made in the first half of Feb.

The premise of most momentum indicators is that the higher the momentum, the greater the number of candles in a period should have their closing price close to an extreme. In a period of bullish momentum, that means closing price is close to the high, and in bearish momentum, closing price is close to the low.

MACD – Moving Average Convergence Divergence

The MACD is an indicator that helps us decide when to buy, sell or hold a particular stock, and gives us a picture of the health of a trend.

The MACD calculates the difference between a 12-day EMA and a 26-day EMA and plots it underneath the trading chart as an oscillator to determine the trend. This resulting line is referred to as simply the MACD line. A 9-day EMA called the signal line, and a histogram that looks like a bar-chart; visually showing the difference between the MACD and the signal line are both also plotted.

Fig. 68: *Microsoft (MSFT) H1 2022 (May-Jun) with the MACD applied. The MACD line is light grey, and the signal line is dark grey. Positive histogram values are light grey, whereas negative histogram values are dark grey.*

The MACD is a momentum indicator that is the rate of change of the two MAs, and therefore more receptive to short-term trends.

If the MACD line is bullish and positive (above the baseline), it means the 12-day EMA is getting further from the 26-day EMA and therefore the price has bullish momentum. Conversely, if the MACD line is bearish and negative (below the baseline), it means the 12-day EMA is getting further from the 26-day EMA and therefore the price has bearish momentum. The steepness of the MACD line can indicate how fast prices are rising or falling. The histogram shows traders the rate of change in price, the larger the difference between a MACD and signal line – represented by larger histogram bars - the greater the rate of momentum of price action. Shorter histogram bars could hint at a trend reversal.

The buy and sell signals from the MACD are very similar to the MA - when the MACD line (light grey) crosses above the signal line (dark grey), this is a buy signal. When the MACD line crosses below the signal line, this is a sell signal.

Because the MACD line reacts immediately to changes in the rate of price movement and is compared to a short 9-day EMA, investors can make buy sell decisions sooner than the equivalent crossovers of the two MAs in the previous chapter.

The clarity of the crossover is correlated with the strength of the signal. If the MACD and signal line clearly cross over, then this is stronger signal than a MACD line that slowly crosses over, such as the crossovers at the 18th and 24th May in the trading chart above.

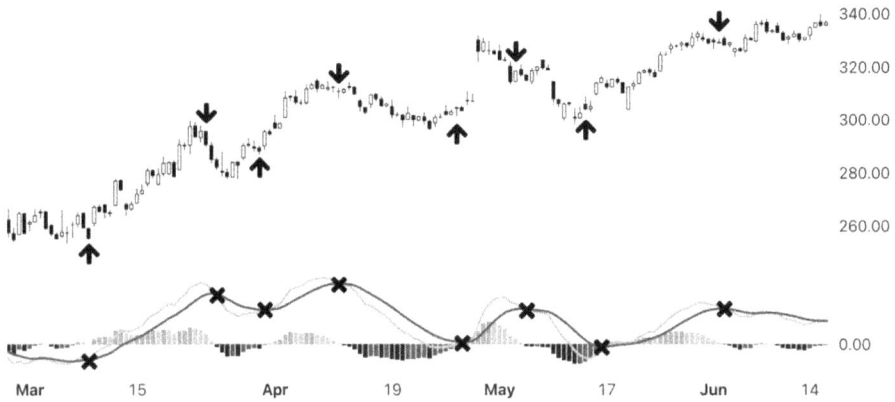

Fig. 69: *Meta (META) H4 2021 (Mar-Jun) with the MACD applied and a series of crossovers annotated with the corresponding buy signals (up arrows) and sell signals (down arrows).*

In Fig. 69, META is shown following a bullish pattern. The MACD here shows a series of buy and sell signals via relatively clear crossovers. Note how the lines in the indicator generally remain above the baseline, confirming that the longer-term trend here is bullish.

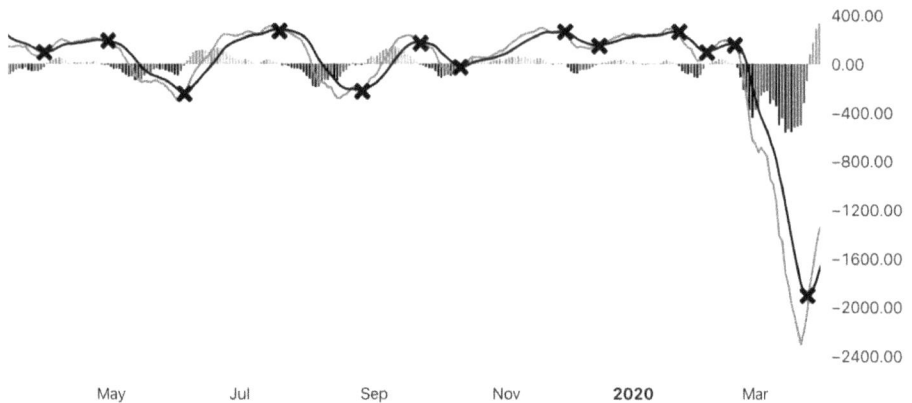

Fig. 70: *Dow Jones Industrial Average (DJI) D1 2019-2020 (Apr-Mar). The MACD with a 12 and 26-day EMA MACD line (light grey), a 9-day EMA (dark grey), and a histogram plotted. MACD and signal line crossovers are annotated by a cross, along with the corresponding buy signals (up arrow) and sell signals (down arrows).*

Looking at how the MACD offers traders signals sooner than the MA crossovers, we have taken the same chart from Fig. 65 and added signals provided by the MACD in Fig. 70. Whilst the moving average does provide some good buy signals (when price touches the MA support levels), the MAs are slow to indicate a trend reversal, and the death cross only occurs after the dip has been passed.

The MACD on the other hand also provides a series of good buy and sell signals (highlighted as arrows on the trading chart) but warns us of the trend reversal a lot sooner than the MAs. Initially, at the last bullish momentum of February 2020, the histogram bars are short and bullish momentum seems weak. The crossover of the MACD and signal line signaling a trend reversal occurs near peak price, although the crossover is not as super-clear as some of the others.

To confirm the trend reversal, we can also look at the lines and the bars. The bars get longer as the market starts to crash. The MACD line and signal line also start to crash towards the baseline soon after the MACD trend reversal, confirming the bearish trend reversal, before the price even comes close to the death cross on the two MAs.

The MACD, as well as providing buy and sell signals, can also alert us of the strength of a trend.

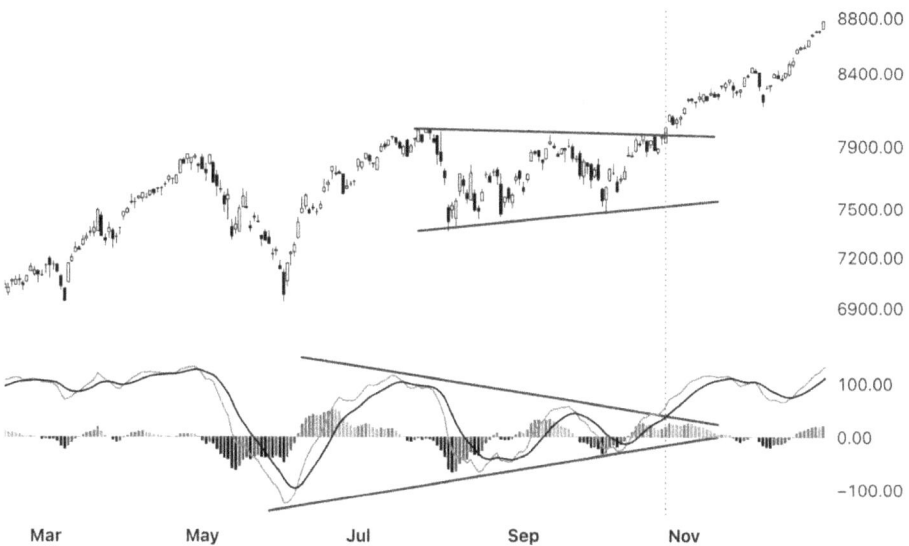

Fig. 71: *Nasdaq 100 (NDQ) D1 2019 (Feb-Dec) with the MACD applied and a triangle pattern annotated on both price and MACD.*

Here, in Fig. 71, we see NDQ consolidating within a symmetrical triangle pattern. A quick look at the MACD shows us that both

MACD and signal line are also consolidating, such that we can draw a similar symmetrical triangle pattern on the MACD indicator. We see a breakout to the upside on NDQ, and on the same trading day, we also get a confirmation from the MACD as the signal line has already broken out above the resistance. The MACD line also confirms this soon after. The MACD and price may exhibit a delay before both confirm, for example, the price may break out of a pattern and the MACD confirms this a few trading days later. The trader may choose to enter the trade on the price breakout if there is enough other evidence to support the breakout or choose to wait for the MACD to confirm.

Fig. 72: *Roblox Corp. (RBLX) D1 2021-2022 (Oct-Aug) with the MACD applied.*

In Fig. 72, RBLX can be seen here in a bearish trend, with clear lower lows defined by the bearish trendline. Yet, a glance at the

MACD reveals a whole different story. Whilst the price is making lower lows, the MACD in the same timeframe is making higher lows, defined by the bullish trendline. This is a bullish divergence, and a hint that the bearish trend may change in the future. Indeed, after a few months, we see RBLX begin on a new bullish trend.

In summary, MACD is good for confirming changes in trend and the momentum of any given trend. There are multiple signals, the clarity of the crossover, the size of the histogram bars, and the bullish and bearish MACD line movement that allow traders to get a feel for the momentum of the trend, as well as trend reversals. When combined with other indicators, traders can get even more confirmations on buy and sell signals and trend reversals.

No indicator is perfect, however, MACD is one of the clearest indicators for buy sell signals and a very popular one amongst professional traders and investors, and overall scores highly for reliability.

RSI – Relative Strength Index

The RSI is a technical indicator that is great at showing the momentum of the stock and the trend it is following. Similar to how we use volume to determine the strength of a trend, the RSI can be used alongside volume to give us even more confidence in that trend.

RSI works by taking the average gain or loss of each candle over a given period, the default being 14 candles. The exact formula for the RSI is:

RSI = 100 - [100 / (1 + RS)]

Where:

RS = Average of x periods up close / Average of x period down close

Where x = number of periods.

The result is an indicator that gives us a number from 0 to 100 and that is the scale for how overbought or oversold a stock is, with 0 being completely oversold and 100 being completely overbought. The higher the average gains over the given period, the higher the RSI value and vice versa. The value for RSI will change retroactively, and so the RSI value is plotted as a line called the RSI line over time. Using the RSI line, we can determine different buy and sell signals.

The trading chart below is of AAPL with the RSI indicator positioned underneath. On the RSI graph, you can see the 0 to 100 scale, and 2 straight lines, one at 30 and one at 70. At an RSI of 30 or less, the stock is considered oversold and when the RSI passes 70, the stock is considered overbought.

When the RSI line passes 70 and becomes overbought, this is a sign that it is unsustainably bullish, may soon be running out of momentum and unlikely to be bullish for much longer. An RSI line of under 30 in the oversold region is a sign that it is unsustainably bearish, may soon be running out of momentum and won't be bearish for much longer. An RSI of 70 or above is therefore a good opportunity to sell and an RSI of under 30 is a good opportunity to buy.

Fig. 73: *H4 of Nvidia (NVDA) 2021 (Jul-Sept) with the RSI applied and oversold/overbought crossings with corresponding buy signals (up arrows) and sell signals (down arrows) annotated.*

In Fig. 73, you can see NVDA decline in July 2021 with the RSI initially above 70 in overbought territory. The sell signal from the RSI comes when the value of the RSI drops below 70. NVDA then drops from $200 to around $180 where the RSI becomes briefly oversold at a value below 30 before rising again. Leaving the oversold zone prompting a buy signal, NVDA goes on to steadily climb up to around $225, where we get the RSI leaving the overbought zone and prompting a sell signal – leaving the trader who used the RSI to trade at $180 a handsome 25% profit on NVDA.

In another example of the RSI, the trading chart in Fig. 74 is TSLA stock in 2019. You can see a large oversold area in May 2019. The stock is no longer oversold at the start of June, indicating a buy signal. Fast forward to the end period of the overbought region at the end of 2019, this is a good sell signal, and if we would have followed the RSI alone, we would have been up around 60-70% from TSLA.

Fig. 74: *Tesla Inc. (TSLA) D1 in 2019 (May-Jul) with the RSI applied and oversold/overbought crossings with corresponding buy signals (up arrows) and sell signals (down arrows) annotated.*

The RSI is also a useful indicator for showing us the momentum of a given trend. In a similar manner to how we use price-volume analysis to assess the balance of buyers and sellers in the market, we can use RSI to determine whether a trend is set to continue, or if there are technical weaknesses suggesting a reversal may come soon.

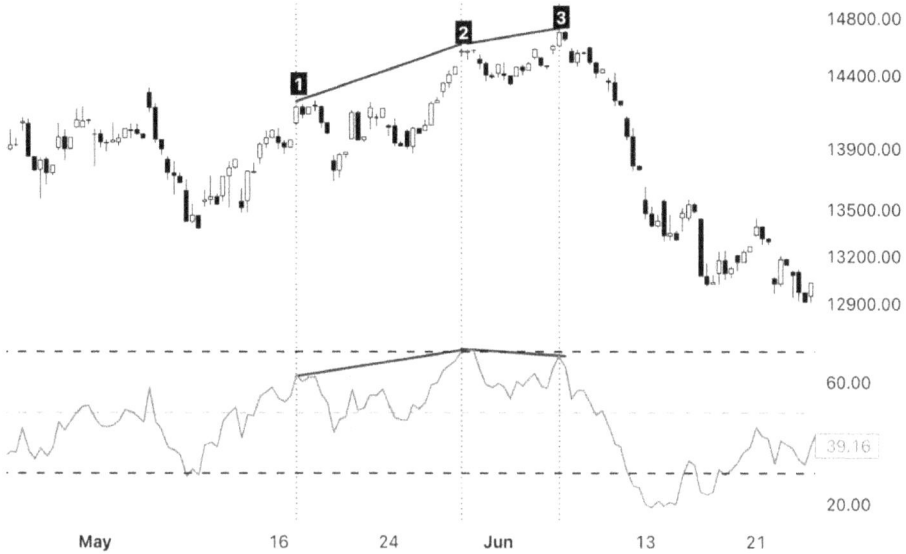

Fig. 75: *DAX Index (DEU40) H4 2022 (Apr-Jun) with the RSI applied and trendlines connecting highs.*

In Fig. 75, showing the German Market Index (Deutsches Aktien Index), the index forms a high at around 14200 pts (labelled 1) before a pullback and a higher high (labelled 2). This higher high on the DAX is confirmed by the RSI, which also produces a higher high. This price to RSI relationship is a normal one as they both confirm each other. However, when the DAX pulls back and goes for another higher high (labelled 3), notice how the RSI fails to produce a higher high. The corresponding trendline connecting high 2 and 3 on the DAX slopes upwards, but on the RSI, the trendline slopes down. This difference is a divergence, which indicates weakness in a trend, in this case, the prevailing uptrend, and hints to us that a change of trend may be around the corner. Indeed, after the higher high at 3, the DAX begins it decline that continues throughout June. Another confirming sign in this case would also be the DAX falling below a support trendline connecting the lows throughout May. Can you spot what I am talking about?

The RSI can also form patterns that can help us confirm emerging price patterns.

Fig. 76: *BTC/USDT D1 2022 (Jun – Sept) with the RSI applied and a rising wedge pattern annotated on both price and RSI.*

In Fig. 76, BTC/USDT exhibits a rising wedge forming throughout the end of July and into August. A quick glance of the RSI doesn't give us a clear divergence when we connect the highs, but what it does give us is a similar pattern to that found on the BTC/USDT price. The fact that the RSI is also showing us a pattern adds conviction to the subsequent breakout to the downside, and in this case, the breakout for the price and the RSI occurs within 1 trading day of each other. Trendline breaks on the RSI do not have to occur at the same time, the RSI can confirm a breakout day or even weeks before or after a trendline breakout on the price.

Fig. 77: *Tesla Inc. (TSLA) D1 2022 - 2023 (Jul-Feb) with the RSI applied and the down trendlines annotated.*

In Fig. 77, both the price and the RSI follow a downtrend, visualized by two similar bearish trendlines. The price reaches $100 before bouncing. The RSI down trendline is broken first, suggesting a change of trend is occurring. However, a trader would approach with caution as the bearish price trendline is yet to be broken at this point. Upon a continued bounce, the price trendline finally confirms a breakout nearly two weeks after the RSI has confirmed it. Both price and RSI have confirmed the reversal, and a trader can be more confident in the ensuing uptrend. Notice that the day the price pushes above the bearish price trendline, there is a breakout gap – another strong piece of evidence supporting the prospects of the new bullish trend.

The RSI divergences also works in a general downtrend, such as one demonstrated below.

Fig. 78: *Netflix Inc. (NFLX) D1 2021- 2022 (Dec-Aug) with the RSI applied and a rising wedge pattern annotated on both price and RSI.*

Here in Fig. 78, we see NFLX rapidly declining in price throughout the first half of 2022. Whilst the price is making much lower lows from 1 to 2, the RSI makes higher lows in the same period, showing us a big divergence between price and RSI. Furthermore, between 2 and 3, NFLX continues to make lower lows, but the RSI makes a higher low with a steeper trendline than the previous higher low. This shows us that the bearish trend is quickly running out of steam and a reversal to a more bullish trend should come in the near future. What results after the divergence is the NFLX bottoms at around $170 and then changes from a down trend to consolidating in a sidewards trend, before then beginning an uptrend in August. Using the RSI to spot divergences, we foresaw the growing weakness in NFLX's downward towards mid-2022 and had we entered a position anytime between May-July 2022, when several other indicators confirmed this reversal, we would have seen our position increase about 100% as NFLX continued its uptrend to a lofty $360 by January 2023, beautifully closing the enormous gap created in April 2022!

In summary the RSI is great for giving us by and sell signals and gauging the momentum of the stock and works especially well when used in combination with trendlines and the MACD indicator.

Stochastic Oscillator

The Stochastic Oscillator, as with other oscillators, generates overbought and oversold signals. The stochastic oscillator takes the closing price of an asset and compares that price to the market price over a given timeframe, which is typically 14 days.

The calculation for the value of the stochastic oscillator is:

Stochastic oscillator = (Closing price – L) / (H – L) x 100.

Where the stochastic oscillator is a value between 0 to 100,

H = Highest price in a 14-day period and L = Lowest Price in a 14-day period

If the market price is close to the highest traded market prices, at 80 or above, there will be overbought signals, and if market price is close to the lowest traded market prices, at 20 or below, there will be oversold signals. The stochastic oscillator comes with 2 lines, one with the current closing price that produces sharper movements, and the other line a smoother one with a 3-day closing price average.

The Stochastic oscillator theorizes that the closing price should be close to the average market price in each trend, making it a great indicator to use when the market is trending sideways and choppy. Therefore, we often switch from an indicator such as the RSI in trending markets, to the Stochastic Oscillator when a trading range has been confirmed.

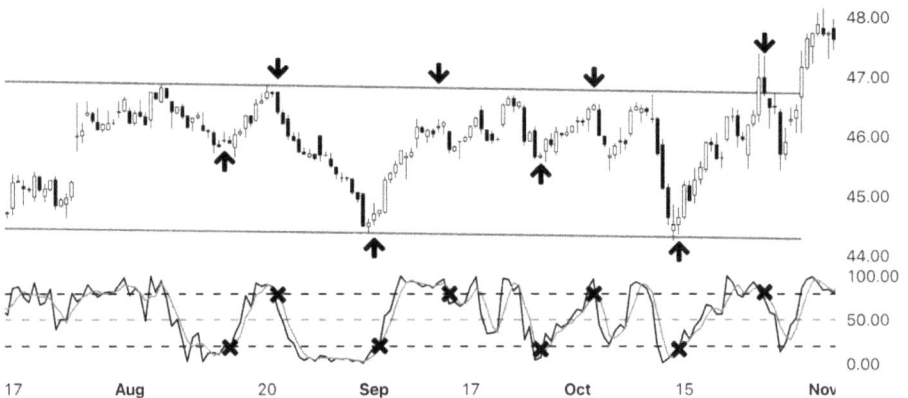

Fig. 79: *Coca Cola (KO) H4 2018 (Jul-Oct) with the stochastic oscillator applied. Buy signals on the oscillator is crossed, and the corresponding signals on price arrowed.*

In Fig. 79, KO is trending sideways, bouncing between a line of support and resistance, and the oscillator shows good buy and sell signals (crossed) when both lines stop being overbought or oversold, even showing signals when the price has not reached or exceeded the level of support and resistance.

MFI – Money Flow Index

The Money Flow Index (MFI) is a technical indicator that uses both price and volume data to measure buying and selling pressure. The MFI is a close relative to the RSI and may be thought of as a volume-weighted RSI.
The MFI is calculated by combining price and volume data to generate a ratio that reflects the strength of buying or selling pressure in the market.

The MFI is calculated using the following formula:

MFI = 100 - [100 / (1 + Money Flow Ratio)]

Where:
Money Flow Ratio = (Positive Money Flow / Negative Money Flow)

Positive Money Flow is the sum of the money flow on days when the price of the security is higher than the previous day's close, and Negative Money Flow is the sum of the money flow on days when the price of the security is lower than the previous day's close.

The money flow is calculated by multiplying the typical price (average of high, low, and close) by the volume traded on a given day. This value is then compared to the previous day's money flow to determine whether it is positive or negative.

Just like the RSI, the MFI is a bounded oscillator that ranges from 0 to 100. Readings above 80 are considered overbought, while readings below 20 are considered oversold. The most useful application of the MFI is in spotting divergences and confirming patterns and breakouts.

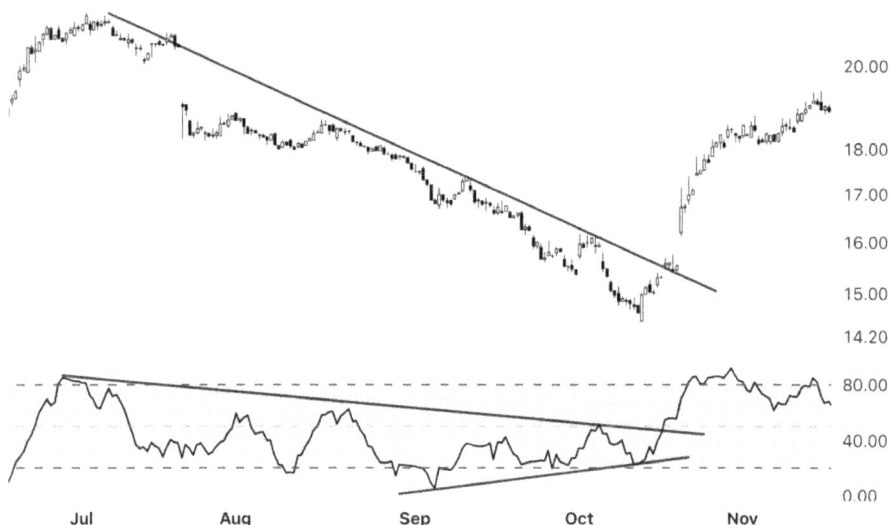

Fig. 80: *AT&T (T) D1 2022 (Jun-Nov) with the MFI applied and corresponding trendlines annotated.*

Here in Fig. 80, we see a steep decline in price, a trend visualized by the trendline. The MFI confirms this trendline by showing us a similar trendline, allowing us to use the MFI to confirm any price breakout from the trendline. Additionally, the MFI shows a bullish divergence, where the price makes lower lows throughout Sept & Oct, and yet the MFI is making higher lows, visualized by the ascending support trendline. This two-fold application of the MFI builds conviction to a trend reversal when the down trendline is broken through. Indeed, a breakout does occur in mid-October, with both price and MFI confirming on the same trading day. The price is initially hesitant to continue up for the following few trading days, but the MFI is already well on its way up above 50. The price retests the down-trendline once more before opening the next trading day with a gap up and a 10% rally over the following week.

Price Rate of Change (ROC)

The Price Rate of Change (ROC) is a technical analysis tool that measures the percentage change in the price of a security over a specified period of time. The ROC is used to identify the strength and direction of price movements and can be used to identify potential trend reversals or confirm the strength of a current trend.

The ROC is calculated using the following formula:

ROC = [(Price today - Price of the security X periods ago) / Price of the security X periods ago] x 100

Where "X" represents the number of periods used in the calculation, where the default period used is 14 days.

The ROC is a bounded oscillator that ranges from negative to positive values. Typically, readings above zero are considered bullish, while readings below zero are considered bearish, and a zero crossover may alert traders that the trend is changing. However, this observation can often produce false signals, called whipsaws, and therefore the strongest use for the ROC is confirming trendline breaks and spotting divergences.

Fig. 81: *General Motors (GM) D1 2022 (Apr-Aug) with the ROC applied.*

Here in Fig. 81, we see a potential falling wedge on the price, and to confirm, we can observe the activity of the ROC. The ROC shows us a similar pattern, a triangle, that we can observe alongside the falling wedge on the price for any breakouts. Furthermore, the support trendline on both price and ROC show a bullish divergence, supporting the bullish implication of a falling wedge. The support trendline on price in down-trending, whereas the support trendline on the ROC is up-trending. Indeed, what transpires is a breakout on GM, confirmed by both ROC and price on the same trading day. A buy upon the breakout would have been a sweet 20% trade in one month.

Mean Reversion Indicators

Mean reversion is a statistical approach to technical analysis of the market. Mean reversion indicators place a presumption on the theory that over time, any divergence of price from the mean will revert to the mean over time. For example, if you do a coin flip 10 tens and record the results, the chances of 5 heads and 5 tails (the statistical average) are not big. However, given enough people to do the same and record the results, the data has a central tendency to the average (5 heads and 5 tails), and this same premise is presumed in price data from the markets. Deviations from the average (result consisting of more than 5 heads, or difference in market price and the moving average) should eventually correct over time.

Fibonacci Retracement Levels

Fibonacci retracement is an indicator that can signal where lines of support and resistance might occur. The Fibonacci Retracement is manually drawn onto a trading chart and based on two points representing a price movement.
For example, if the price increased from $100 to $120, we could plot the Fibonacci retracement with point A being $100 and point

B being $120. The chart would then automatically fill in the Fibonacci Retracement levels which are 23.6%, 38.2%, 50%, 61.8%, and 78.6%.

These percentages are of the price difference between point A and point B – in this case $20. If the price peaked at $120 and is decreasing from the $120 mark, we could see a level of support (and resistance) at any of the Fibonacci Levels, at $115.28 (23.6% decline), $112.36 (38.2% decline), $110 (50% decline), $107.64 (61.8% decline) or $104.28 (78.6% decline).

In Fig. 82, the S&P 500 Index is displayed during the 2020 Stock Market Crash, and a Fibonacci Retracement is drawn from the peak of the market in February, at 3394 pts, to the trough in March at 2193 pts. The Fibonacci retracement levels are automatically plotted and display the price at each of the retracement levels, each of which form a support or resistance level at least once.

As the price of the S&P 500 Index recovered, the price bounced off the retracement levels to varying degrees of precision, making them good places to potentially take profit (at a resistance) or add to a position (at a support).

Fig. 82: *S&P 500 Index (SPX) D1 2020 (Jan-Aug) recovering after the 2020 Stock Market Crash. The Fibonacci Retracement Levels are plotted and show the support and resistance levels of the price recovery.*

In Fig. 83, TSLA is shown from 2017 to January 2023. TSLA experienced a massive rally beginning with the final retest of the line of support at $11.90 and ending at $400 at the end of 2021. The Fibonacci retracement levels are drawn from the swing low at $11.90, to the swing high at $400, and they reveal levels of support and resistance. As TSLA began to lose ground in the wake of economic uncertainty starting in 2022, the Fibonacci levels can show investors and traders potential areas where TSLA may find a support. Note the significance of the 0.236 and the 0.382 Fibonacci levels in January 2023, the latest candle. The price finds a low just below the 0.382 at $105.30 and find a high just above the 0.216 at $176.49.

If TSLA starts heading down in February 2023 onwards, we can state, using evidence from the fib levels, that TSLA may reasonably find support at $105.30, but if that Fibonacci level is lost, then the next support is $69.36 at the 0.5 Fibonacci level.

Fig. 83: *Tesla Inc. (TSLA) Mo1 2017-2023 with Fibonacci Retracement Levels added.*

As well as forecasting retracement levels for a correction or trend reversal, the Fibonacci levels can also be used in forecasting potential support and resistance levels if prices continue to rise (or fall in a downtrend).

Taking a closer look at TSLA in Fig. 84, for the same rally, we have now drawn the Fibonacci levels from the first rally from $11.93 to $65.01, representing the swing low and high respectively. The following retracement during the pandemic shock tested the 0.382 at $22.78 before the rally ensued.

The levels 1.272, 1.618 and 2 are also added as future levels to watch out for in the case TSLA continued its rally past the swing high at $65.01. These levels are derived by dividing 1 by the Fibonacci levels 0.764, 0.618 and 0.5 respectively, and note how price interacts with the forward-looking Fibonacci levels, as highlighted below with arrows.

Fig. 84: *Tesla Inc. (TSLA) W1 2018-2023 (Dec-Feb) with Fibonacci Retracement & Extension Levels added.*

Bollinger Bands

The Bollinger Bands are a more recent technical analysis tool that extends the utility of the MA (typically the 20-day SMA) by plotting 2 standard deviations, one on the positive side of the MA, and one on the negative side. It therefore encompasses of 3 lines (bands) that are overlaid onto the trading chart.

The outer bands of the Bollinger Bands function like the RSI, in that they alert traders on when a stock might be overbought and oversold.

When the price movement is continuously touching the upper band, this could indicate that the stock is overbought, and may be a sell signal. When the price movement is continuously touching the bottom band, this means that the stock is oversold and may be a buy signal. Since 95% of price action occurs within 2 standard deviations, a price move outside these bands is a very visual cue that can be considered a large event. In such occurrences, other indicators should then be used to confirm any buy or sell signals.

Fig. 85: *Walt Disney Co. (DIS) H4 2021 (Jul-Oct) with 20-day Bollinger Bands added.*

The Bollinger Bands are used for analyzing short-term price movements since standard deviation is a measure of volatility. Volatility is a statistical measure of how much prices fluctuates from the average.

The distance between the two bands represents the level of volatility. If the bands are getting wider, the volatility of the price is increasing, and if the bands are getting narrower, the volatility is decreasing, and when particularly narrow and close to the MA, a feature called the squeeze can signal increased volatility and trading opportunities ahead.

Fig. 86: *ETH/USDT D1 2021 (Jul-Oct) with 20-day Bollinger Bands added.*

Here in Fig. 86, we can see that ETH/USDT drastically reduces in volatility in October, leading into a squeeze where the outer bands of the Bollinger Bands are considerably closer than any time prior. We see that after nearly three weeks of low volatility, the price finally tests and penetrates the upper bands with the largest candles we have seen since prior to the squeeze, alerting traders that there are likely going to be more large price movements ahead.

Bollinger Bands can also help us see the larger trends at play, and smooth out any very-short term noise in a way similar to MAs. Just like trendlines and identifying trading channels, Bollinger Bands can paint a picture of where markets are trending. They fall short when confirming trend reversals however, since the MA and bands are smoothed and are relatively slow to react.

Linear Regression Channel

The Linear Regression Channel is a technical analysis tool that is used to identify trends in the price. A trader can use linear regression channels by plotting a straight line that best fits the price data over a specific time period, typically from a low to a high of a given trend. The channel is used to identify potential support and resistance levels, as well as to identify potential trend reversals.

The Linear Regression Channel is created by calculating the linear regression line for a specific period of time. This line is then used as the centerline for the channel. The upper and lower lines of the channel are two standard deviations away from the centerline as default.

The Linear Regression Channel can be used to identify potential support and resistance levels in each trend. When the price reaches the upper line, it could signal that prices are overbought and provide a sell signal, and likewise when the price touches the lower line, it could signal that prices are oversold and provide a buy signal.

The linear regression channel is also great at determining whether the current trend is intact, or if there is a new trend in play.

Fig. 87: *UK100 Index (UKX) D1 2022-2023 (Sept-Mar) with the linear regression channel applied from Oct 13 to Feb 16.*

In Fig. 87, the UKX index has a linear regression channel applied to the bullish trend that begins with the low in October, all the way to high in February. Notice how the price bounces from the lower support line and the upper resistance line multiple times throughout this uptrend. Some tests of the support and resistance provide good entry and exit signals in the uptrend, although other tests provide false signals – highlighting the importance of using multiple technical methods to confirm an entry and exit.

The linear regression channel also clearly highlights when the bullish trend has come to an end. In February, we can see that price comes to the support line and remains there before decisively breaking below the support at the beginning of March. This makes linear regression channels one in your arsenal of indicators that can identify and pinpoint trend reversals.

Market Breadth Indicators

Market breadth indicators are technical analysis tools that measure the overall strength and participation of stocks in a market index or exchange. The premise of these indicators is that a healthy market is typically characterized by broad participation, with most stocks moving in the same direction as the primary trend of the market. For example, if the S&P 500 were to follow a bullish trend, we would expect to see most U.S. stocks (statistically about 75%) follow suit in this bullish move. Conversely, if the S&P 500 were to make a bullish move, and most stocks failed to make a bullish move, this divergence suggests that just a few large stocks are driving the major average and that can be interpreted as market weakness and that a change of trend may be coming. Market breadth indicators are not buy or sell signals, and are not good at timing the markets. They can hint at potential reversals, but often, the market can continue in its current trend for weeks and even months after a divergence is shown. Traders should also use other indicators and trendlines to confirm buy and sell signals.

Advance / Decline Index (A/D Line)

The Advance/Decline Index, also known as the A/D Line or Breadth Indicator, is a widely used technical analysis tool that measures the overall market breadth. It helps traders and investors gauge the market's overall strength and direction by comparing the number of advancing stocks (those with higher closing prices) to the number of declining stocks (those with lower closing prices) in a specific market index or exchange.

The Advance/Decline Index is calculated by taking the difference between the number of advancing and declining stocks and then adding the result to the previous value of the index. This creates a cumulative line that can be charted over time:

Advance/Decline Index = (Advancing Stocks - Declining Stocks) + Previous A/D Index Value

As with other types of technical indicators, the A/D Line can be used to assess the strength of the current trend and can also be annotated with trendlines and patterns to confirm price breakouts and trend reversals.

Fig. 88: *S&P 500 Index (SPX) H1 2022 (Jun-Jul) with the Advance Decline Line applied and divergences annotated.*

In Fig. 88, the A/D Line is applied to the SPX where in most cases, the A/D Line follows the same direction as the price. Therefore, when there is a divergence, it tends to stick out like a sore thumb, making the A/D line one of my preferred tools for assessing the trend in the SPX. The price advances throughout the beginning of July, but the A/D line declines. This divergence is not an immediate sell signal, and one should use this in conjunction with other indicators to confirm, but on this occasion, the rally ends and completely retraces prior gains.

High-Low Index

The high-low index is a technical analysis tool used by traders to measure market momentum and identify potential trend reversals. It is calculated by dividing the number of new 52-week highs by the number of new 52-week lows on a given stock exchange, and then plotting the result on a chart.

The high-low index is used to identify the strength of a market trend. If the high-low index is high, it indicates that there are more new highs than new lows, which suggests a strong uptrend in the market. Conversely, if the high-low index is low, it indicates that there are more new lows than new highs, which suggests a strong downtrend in the market.

Fig. 89: *S&P 500 Index (SPX) D1 2022-2023 (Oct-Mar) with the NYSE New Highs Index applied and the extreme reading annotated.*

The High-Low index in Fig. 89 measures how many stocks are making a new high. An extreme reading in the high-low index can be interpreted as an oversold market and can be a good contrarian signal. In this example, the extreme reading in the

High-Low Index on the SPX resulted in a market decline over the following month.

S&P 500 Stocks Above X-Day MA Index

This indicator is another useful market breadth indicator that measures the number of stocks as a proportion to total stocks above their respective moving average (MA). Remember that stocks above their MA are generally in a bullish trend and stocks below their MA are in a bearish trend – so the premise with this indicator is the same as the previous two indicators discussed.

This indicator can be used for any MA length, but the most popular being the S&P 500 Stocks Above 200-Day MA index as that is an indication of where stocks are in the primary trend. Other useful ones are the 50-day MA index for intermediate trends, and 20-day MA index for short-term trends.

In Fig. 90, we can see the SPX makes a high at the beginning of 2018 before a crash. The SPX recovers and successfully creates a new high by September 2018, but both the 50-day and 200-day MA indices fail to confirm the higher high, instead posting a lower high and creating a divergence. Not long after, the rally abruptly reverses, and the SPX experiences a 20% drop in the following 2 months!

Fig. 90: *S&P 500 Index (SPX) W1 2017-2019 (Sept-Jan) with both S&P 500 Stocks Above 200-Day MA Index (black) and S&P 500 Stocks Above 50-Day MA Index (grey) applied and divergences annotated.*

Relative Strength

Relative strength shows us how well an asset is performing compared to a benchmark or other assets. Not to be confused with the Relative Strength Index (RSI) indicator, the Relative Strength compares the performance of an asset by the S&P 500 by default. If the asset is underperforming, the value of relative will be less than 0, and if it is outperforming, then its value will be above 0.

The relative strength can show us how different assets behave in different trends of the market, as well as changes in regards in this performance.

Fig. 91: *Block Inc. (SQ) W1 2019-2021 (Oct-Oct) with the RS applied.*

Here in Fig. 91, we can see SQ initially starts weaker than the performance of the S&P 500 at the first arrow in 2020. However, SQ performances increasingly outperforms the S&P, demonstrated by the bullish trendline on the RS. This increasing RS is what we want to look for when buying stocks or other investments.

The RS then breaks down below the trendline in the start of 2021, confirmed a few months later in the price. At this point (second arrow), we get a sell signal. The RS remains above 0 throughout the rest of 2021, meaning that SQ still outperforms the S&P, but the fact that the value of RS is declining here tells us that SQ is decreasingly outperforming the S&P and losing momentum in that regard. It tells us that there are better opportunities elsewhere.

Fig. 92: *Meta Inc. (META) W1 2021-2023 (Apr-Oct) with the RS applied.*

In an opposite example, META in Fig. 92 can be seen increasingly underperform the S&P, visualized by the bearish trendline on the RS. A similar bearish trendline can also be observed on the price. A breakout occurs on the RS trendline first at start of 2023, followed by a breakout of the price trendline a few weeks later, marking a great buy signal for META when price confirms the RS breakout.

The RS can be further optimized to understand the performance of a stock relative to a specific benchmark, such as its industry or sector. In this way, we can choose the best investments within an industry or sector we think will do well.

The properties of the RS make it ideal for stock selection, its use can be practically applied when we discuss stock selection via the Wyckoff Method later in this book.

Indicator Innovation

We have covered the commonly used indicators and how they are able to show us the technical picture of an investment. However, there are new indicators being introduced into the trading world that may show a greater wealth of information in one indicator, or present traders with buy or sell signals. These indicators tend to blend or build on several other technical indicators.

Fig. 93: *Amazon (AMZN) D1 2018-2019 (Sep-Jan) with a custom indicator "Traders Reality" applied.*

This indicator in Fig. 93 for example, called Trader's Reality adds 5 different MAs onto the screen, pivot points and average daily ranges amongst others to create quite a complex looking display. Within most software, a trader can backtest a particular strategy using a single indicator to understand the profitability of such signals, which will be discussed later.

When using niche indicators, make sure to understand what they are trying to show you and how it generates it's buy and sell signals if it has any.
Remember to take any indicator profitability with a pinch of salt. This is because of well-known saying in trading - history never repeats itself, but it rhymes. A well-performing indicator when tested on historical price data is no guarantee of similar results in the future!

TECHNICAL INDICATORS
KEY POINTS:

- **Technical indicators are added to a chart to help give us insight into the current trend, confirm chart patterns and provide buy and sell signals.**

- **Volume indicators shows us where the smart money is and can help us analyze trends, price action and confirm breakouts, price patterns and trend reversals.**

- **The moving average (MA) indicates whether the trend is currently bullish, bearish or sideways. The MA can** be used a dynamic support & resistance and MA crossovers can hint at a trend reversal.

- Momentum indicators show us the momentum behind price action and trends and provide us with overbought and oversold signals. These indicators include the RSI and MACD and can be used to analyze a trend and to confirm breakouts, price patterns and trend reversals.

- Mean reversion indicators posit that price always reverts back to the mean in the long run, so extreme readings often lead back to the mean. Indicators include Fibonacci Retracement Levels and Bollinger Bands.

- Market breadth indicators shows whether the majority of stocks in the market are bullish or bearish, which can help confirm trades.

- Relative strength shows us how well a stock is performing compared to a benchmark.

VI. Advanced Technical Concepts & Trading Strategies

Cycles

In the context of the stock market, cycles refer to recurring patterns of price movement or market behavior that can be observed over time. These cycles often result from various factors, such as economic activity, investor sentiment, and geopolitical events. By understanding and analyzing market cycles, traders and investors can make better-informed decisions and potentially capitalize on opportunities arising from these patterns.

Business Cycle

The business cycle, also known as the economic cycle, refers to the recurring pattern of economic expansion and contraction that occurs in market economies. The business cycle is responsible for the primary trend as identified in the Dow Theory.

The cycle is characterized by fluctuations in economic activity, including changes in employment, production, and income, and a close eye on economic indicators relating to these, as well as technical analysis of the markets can help you understand where in the business cycle we are.

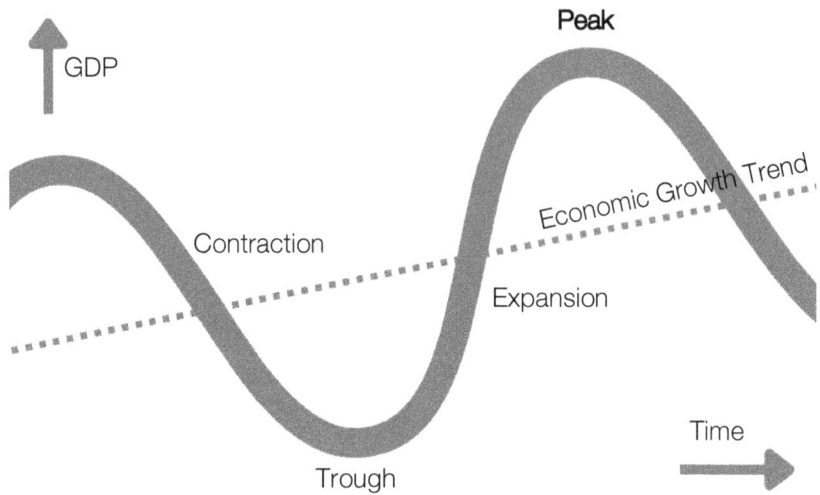

Fig. 94: *The idealized business cycle with the four phases labelled.*

The business cycle typically consists of four stages: expansion, peak, contraction, and trough.

- **Expansion**: This stage is characterized by increasing economic activity, including rising GDP, increasing employment, and expanding business activity. The expansion stage is marked by a period of sustained economic growth, typically lasting several years.

- **Peak**: The peak stage is the point at which the economy reaches its highest point in the business cycle. This is characterized by high levels of economic activity, low unemployment, and high levels of production and consumption. The inflation rate tends to also be soaring, and government intervention by increasing interest rates starts to send the stock market into decline.

- **Contraction**: The contraction stage is marked by a decline in economic activity, including falling GDP, rising unemployment, and declining business activity. This stage is often referred to as a recession or economic downturn.

- **Trough**: The trough stage is the point at which the economy reaches its lowest point in the business cycle. This stage is characterized by low levels of economic activity, high unemployment, and low levels of production and consumption.

After the trough stage, the cycle begins again with a new period of expansion.

The business cycle is influenced by a variety of factors, including monetary policy, fiscal policy, and external shocks such as natural disasters or international conflicts, the details of which are outside the purview of this book.

As a rule of thumb, the S&P 500 stock market index tend to lead the business cycle by 3-6 months, meaning that the stock market low will come 3-6 months before the economy is at worst.

Kondratieff Cycle

The Kondratieff Cycle, also known as the Kondratieff Wave, is a long-term economic cycle that was proposed by Russian economist Nikolai Kondratieff in the early 20th century.

The Kondratieff Cycle is a cycle of about 40-60 years that consists of four phases: the inflationary upswing, the stagflationary downswing, the deflationary depression, and the recovery. Each phase of the cycle is characterized by different economic conditions and trends. The Kondratieff cycle is notable for being a secular long-term trend, with each sub-phase within the 40–60-year supercycle lasting on average anywhere between 8-14 years. It is only when we zoom out on the stock market, particularly that of the S&P 500 does the Kondratieff cycle become apparent.

During the inflationary upswing phase, the economy experiences growth and expansion, which leads to increased inflation and rising interest rates. This phase is typically characterized by increasing business investment, rising stock prices, and a strong economy. This phase is widely believed to begin around 1971 along with Kondratieff's 5th cycle, and around 2010 for the 6th cycle, soon after the 2008 financial crisis.

During the stagflationary downswing phase, the economy experiences slowing growth and rising inflation, which leads to a period of economic stagnation. This phase is typically characterized by high unemployment, falling stock prices, and slow economic growth.

During the deflationary depression phase, the economy experiences a severe contraction, with falling prices, high unemployment, and low economic growth. This phase is typically characterized by a decline in consumer spending and business investment.

Finally, during the recovery phase, the economy begins to recover from the depression, with rising economic growth and falling unemployment. This phase is typically characterized by increasing consumer confidence and a return to economic stability.

Presidential Cycle

The Presidential Cycle, also known as the Presidential Election Cycle or the Four-Year Cycle, refers to the pattern of stock market performance in the United States that is correlated with the four-year presidential term. The cycle is based on the premise that the stock market tends to perform differently during different stages of the presidential term.

The Presidential Cycle typically consists of four stages:

Year 1: The first year of the presidential term is often characterized by a weak stock market, as investors and businesses adjust to new policies and priorities set by the new administration.

Year 2: The second year of the presidential term is often marked by improving economic conditions and a stronger stock market as policies begin to take effect.

Year 3: The third year of the presidential term is typically the strongest for the stock market, as the economy and corporate profits continue to improve. Since 1933, the gains on the S&P 500 in the third year have averaged 16.3%, over double the average of the other 3 years!

Year 4: The fourth year of the presidential term is often marked by a weaker stock market, as investors anticipate changes in policy and potential election uncertainty.

The most reliable takeaway has been that the third year of the four-year cycle has been the strongest performer.

Elliott Wave Theory

The Elliott Wave Theory is a technical analysis approach to predicting stock market movements developed by Ralph Nelson Elliott in the 1930s. It is based on the idea that stock prices move in predictable patterns, which can be analyzed and used to make investment decisions.

The Elliott Wave Theory is based on the premise that stock prices move in five waves in the direction of the trend, known as impulse waves, followed by three corrective waves. These waves can be charted on a price chart and can be used to predict future price movements.

The five impulse waves are labeled 1, 2, 3, 4, and 5. These waves are upward or downward movements in the price of the stock, depending on whether the trend is bullish or bearish. The three corrective waves, labeled A, B, and C, are counter-trend movements that occur between the five waves.

The Elliott Wave Theory also includes several rules and guidelines for identifying and analyzing the waves. When numbering waves in the Elliott Wave Theory, there are several important rules and guidelines that help ensure the correct identification and labeling of the impulse and corrective waves. These rules maintain the consistency and validity of the wave count and help to avoid misinterpretations.

- Wave 2 never retraces more than 100% of Wave 1: In an impulse wave, Wave 2 should never retrace more than the entirety of Wave 1. If the retracement exceeds 100% of Wave 1, it is not a valid Wave 2, and the wave count should be reconsidered.

- Wave 3 is never the shortest impulse wave: Among the three impulse waves (1, 3, and 5), Wave 3 is never the shortest in terms of price distance. While Wave 3 is often the longest and strongest wave, it is not a strict requirement; however, it must never be shorter than both Waves 1 and 5.

- Wave 4 does not overlap with the price territory of Wave 1: In an impulse wave, Wave 4 should not enter the price territory of Wave 1. If there is an overlap between the two waves, it indicates that the wave count is incorrect, and a reassessment is needed.

Fig. 95: *EUR/USD D1 2020-2021 (Apr-Apr) with the Elliott Impulse Wave and Elliott Correction Wave annotated and volume applied.*

In Fig. 95, the EUR/USD is in an uptrend and so the intermediate impulse wave features higher highs and higher lows, followed by the corrective wave. A trader can use the Elliott Wave along with other indicators and chart patterns to gauge the strength of a trend and the likelihood of a trend reversal.

The Elliott Wave makes use of the Fibonacci Retracement Levels, as along with the three rules, there are guidelines to the size of the impulse waves:

- Wave 2 is typically 50%, 61.8%, 76.4%, or 85.4% of wave 1.
- Wave 3 is typically 161.8% the distance of wave 1.
- Wave 4 is typically 14.6%, 23.6%, or 38.2% of wave 3.
- Wave 5 is typically 161.8% the distance of wave 1 and 3 combined.

The corrective waves may manifest themselves in several ways, in Fig. 95, the corrective wave is a zigzag where the condition is Wave C is lower than Wave A, and Wave B is at least 38.2% of the distance of wave A. Another form is a flat, where Wave B must be 61.8% of the distance of wave A, and wave C retraces at least 38.2% of the distance of wave A. In both cases, wave B must not make a new high, i.e., exceed the price of wave 5 in the impulse wave.

These guidelines can help us confirm the existence of such a wave and have forecasting value with respects to the future trend, price movement and expected price target. When combined with other indicators and technical methods, the Elliott Wave can provide great buy and sell signals. Remember though, these are only guidelines and are not required for a valid impulse wave, as you will see in Fig. 96.

To apply the Fibonacci Retracement Levels, when the price begins to retrace from a recent uptrend, draw the Fibonacci Retracement level from point (0) to (1) in Fig. 95, and observe the subsequent retracement. Once the retracement is a confirmed wave 2 according to the rules and guidelines, edit the Fibonacci Retracement levels you have drawn between (0) and (1) to display the extended Fibonacci levels, such as the target, 1.618. It is recommended to add other Fibonacci levels too such as 1.272, 1.414, 2, 2.272 and 2.618 as these may form viable targets for Wave 3. Now observe the price. If there is confirmation from other indicators, now might be a good time to place a long position with the anticipation that price is now in Wave 3. Once wave 3 has completed and a pullback into wave 4 is confirmed, draw the Fibonacci levels between (2) and (3) and look for a pullback to the 0.146, 0.236 or 0.382 Fibonacci level. Finally, once wave 4 has completed and wave 5 is confirmed, draw the Fibonacci Retracement level from (0) to (3) with the same extended Fibonacci levels as wave 3. Observe the price as it approaches any of the extended Fibonacci levels as they could signify the completion of wave 5 and the commencement of a 3-part corrective wave. Wave A is confirmed when wave B surpasses the 0.382 Fibonacci level, which can be drawn between (5) and (A). Wave B must also not exceed the price level of (5). Once wave B is confirmed, wave C should retrace below wave A in a zigzag correction, or at least to the 0.382 Fibonacci level of wave A to be a valid wave C.

Fig. 96: *EUR/USD D1 2020-2021 (Apr-Apr) with the Elliott Impulse Wave and Elliott Correction Wave annotated and select Fibonacci Levels shown.*

In Fig. 96, Wave 2 retraces to exactly the 0.618 Fibonacci level, as per the guideline, giving us conviction to the impulse wave and the subsequent climb in wave 3. Wave 3 does not reach the 1.618 Fibonacci level, instead touching another preset Fibonacci level at 1.272. Although not per the guidelines, the fact that Wave 3 found resistance at any Fibonacci Level is promising. Wave 4 loosely retraces to the 0.618 Fibonacci level, not per guideline but again another valid Fibonacci Level. Wave 5 then extends to another Fibonacci level before completing the impulse wave and starting of the 3-part corrective wave. In summary, the precise pullback of Wave 2 should give a trader using the Elliott Wave

Theory conviction to the rally of Wave 3, and to a lesser extent, Wave 5, and the imminent correction waves.

Above all, the Elliott Wave works with any trend. It can be used to annotate supercycles, which may be years to decades long, to sub-minute trends that happen last just a few minutes. In fact within a wave A of an impulse wave will be an impulse wave on a shorter timeframe trend, and within wave A of that shorter impulse wave will be an impulse wave on an even shorter timeframe trend. In the Elliott Wave theory, the price always moves in waves, also called fractals, whatever timeframe you are on. The Elliott Wave is a truly fascinating method practiced and advocated by millions of traders and investors today.

Selecting The Perfect Investment – The Wyckoff Method

The Wyckoff Method, invented by Richard Wyckoff in the early 20th century, is a technical analysis approach to stock selection that emphasizes the study of price and volume data to identify trends and potential opportunities for buying and selling. Wyckoff listed five steps to selecting any investment:

1. **Identify the overall trend.**

Start by identifying the overall trend of the market, using an index such as the S&P 500. Determine whether it is bullish, bearish, or consolidating within a range. For this, use peak and trough analysis, trendlines, MAs and other trend indicators to determine the trend.

2. **Select stocks moving with the market.**

Look for stocks that outperform the market when the markets are bullish and underperform when the markets are bearish. A great method for this task is the methodology discussed for the relative strength (RS) indicator. Look for a declining value for RS during a bearish market, indicating the stock is increasingly underperforming the market, and look for a rising RS in bullish markets. Assessing the historical RS of stock compared to the market definitely adds a layer of research.

3. Look for accumulation and distribution.

Look for stocks that show considerable accumulation or distribution within the Wyckoff Cycle.

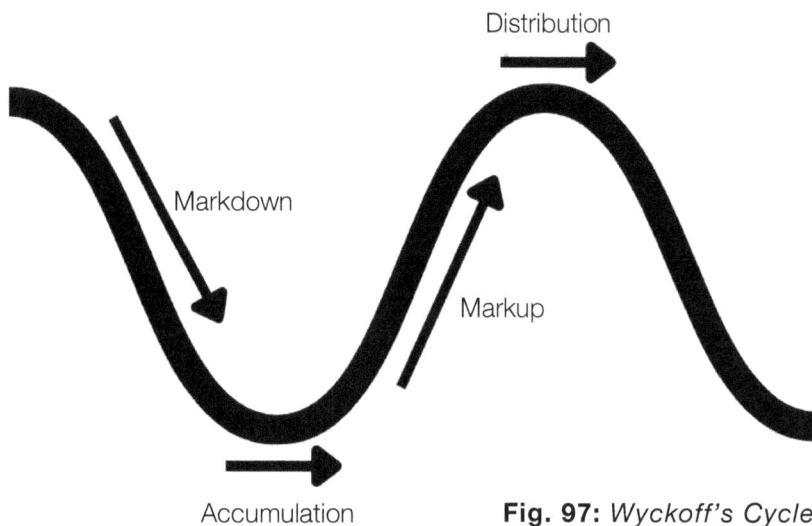

Fig. 97: *Wyckoff's Cycle*

The longer the accumulation or distribution has been occurring, the larger the expected price move in the markup or markdown phases.

4. Determine the stocks readiness to move (markup/markdown).

To determine this, Wyckoff identified notable events across five phases that reveal whether a markup or markdown is ready to occur. In the following accumulation period on EUR/GBP, you will see the nine tests and five phases annotated, and they will be explained on the following page.

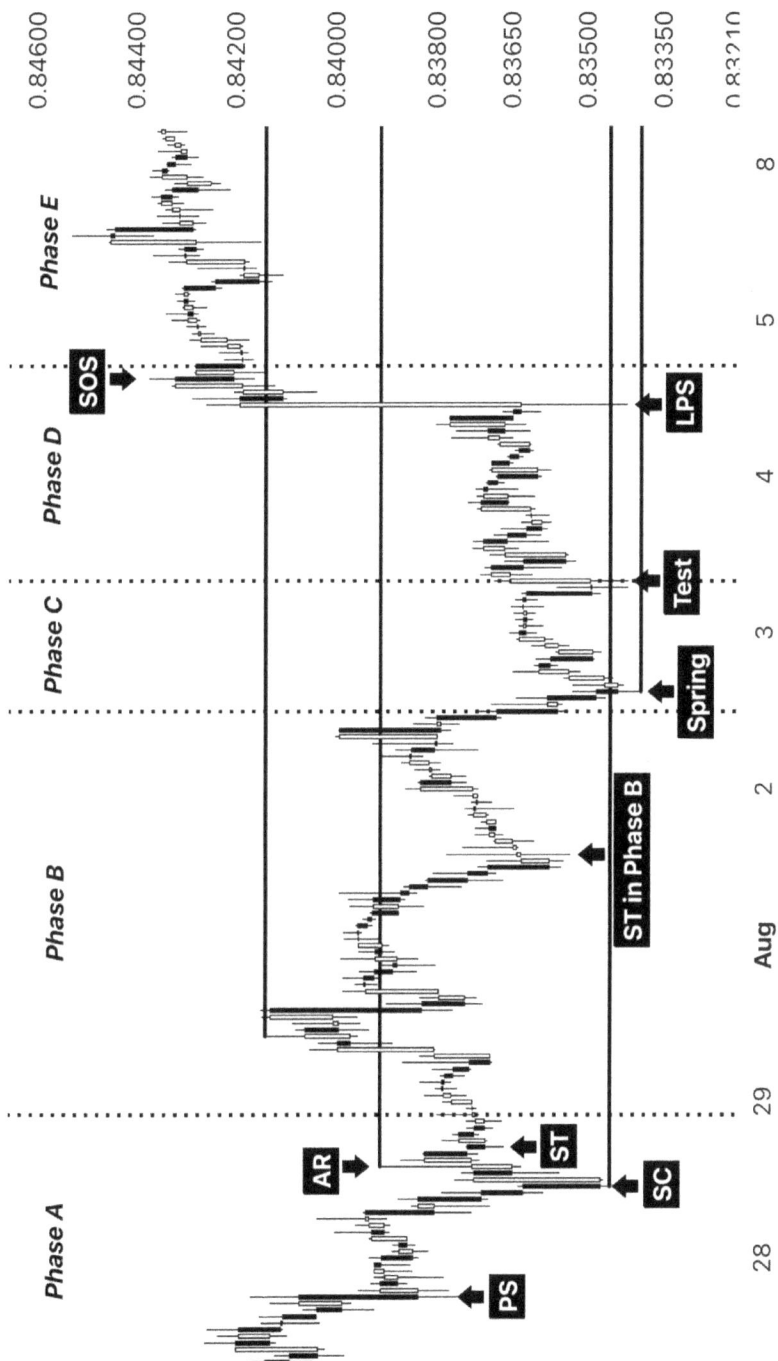

Fig. 98: *EUR/GBP H1 2022 (Jul/Aug) with Wyckoff accumulation events and phases annotated.*

Preliminary Support (PS) - This is the point at which substantial buying begins to emerge, often marked by increased volume and a halt in the price decline.

Selling Climax (SC) - This test involves a sharp drop in price, followed by a sharp rebound, signaling that selling pressure is exhausted and demand is coming back into the market.

Automatic Rally (AR) - After the SC, the price experiences a strong rally on increased demand. The AR creates a resistance level that acts as a reference point for future price action.

Secondary Test (ST) - Following the SC, the market may undergo a secondary test, in which the price declines towards the SC level but with lower volume. This indicates that selling pressure is waning, and the stock is being absorbed by strong hands.

Spring – An optional price move that takes place during Phase C, characterized by a brief dip below the established support of the trading range formed during Phase A or B. The purpose of the Spring is to "shake out" weak hands or late sellers who are still holding on to their positions. This event is usually accompanied by a decline in volume, indicating that selling pressure is waning. The Spring is considered a bullish sign.

Test of Supply - After the ST, the price may experience another decline with reduced volume, but it should hold above the previous lows. This tests the remaining supply and confirms that the stock is being accumulated.

Signs of Strength (SOS) - These are bullish price and volume patterns that confirm accumulation is taking place, such as increased volume on upswings and decreased volume on downswings, and on higher highs.

Last Point of Support (LPS) - The LPS serves as a confirmation that the stock has been successfully accumulated. The LPS is a pullback to a support that was formerly a resistance, on low volume.

To additionally determine if accumulation is occurring, look for the following signs:

- Bullish volume (increases on rallies, decreases on declines
- Downtrending trendline broken
- Higher lows
- Higher Highs
- Stock stronger than the market (increasing Relative Strength)

The five phases can be observed in both accumulation and distribution scenarios. Here, we will discuss the five phases in the context of accumulation; however, the same concepts apply to distribution with opposite price action.

Phase A: Stop the downtrend.

Phase A marks the end of a downtrend and the beginning of the accumulation process. In this phase, key events like Preliminary Support (PS) and Selling Climax (SC) occur. PS represents an initial increase in demand and volume, while SC is characterized by a rapid price decline, followed by a sharp rebound. These events suggest that the market is transitioning from a bearish phase to a more balanced state, where supply and demand begin to stabilize.

Phase B: Building the base.

During Phase B, the stock's price tends to move in a trading range, as the market experiences a period of indecision. This phase can be prolonged and difficult to interpret, as neither the bulls nor bears have complete control. It is characterized by multiple Secondary Tests (ST), where the price revisits the lows established in Phase A but on lower volume. This indicates that selling pressure is diminishing and smart money is quietly accumulating shares.

Phase C: Test of supply.

Phase C is a critical phase in the Wyckoff methodology, as it tests the remaining supply before the markup phase begins. In this phase, the stock price experiences a final decline, known as the "Spring" or "Shakeout," often breaking below the trading range established in Phase B. This event shakes out weak hands, and the decline occurs on lower volume, signaling that the selling pressure is exhausted. After the spring, the price reverses and moves back into the trading range, marking the end of the test.

Phase D: Markup phase

In Phase D, the price begins to trend upward as demand starts to outpace supply. During this phase, traders can observe SOS, such as increased volume on upswings, decreased volume on downswings, and price breakouts from the trading range. As the stock price moves higher, it confirms the successful completion of the accumulation process, and the beginning of a new uptrend.

Phase E: Uptrend acceleration

Phase E is the final phase of the accumulation process, where the stock price accelerates and moves higher in a strong uptrend. In this phase, the stock may experience large price advances on increasing volume, as market participants recognize the strength of the trend and rush to buy shares. The uptrend can continue for an extended period, as the stock reaches new highs and attracts more investors.

The opposite of accumulation is distribution, and the phases of distribution may be known as the opposite of the phases in accumulation. The tests are similar opposites, but are listed for completeness:

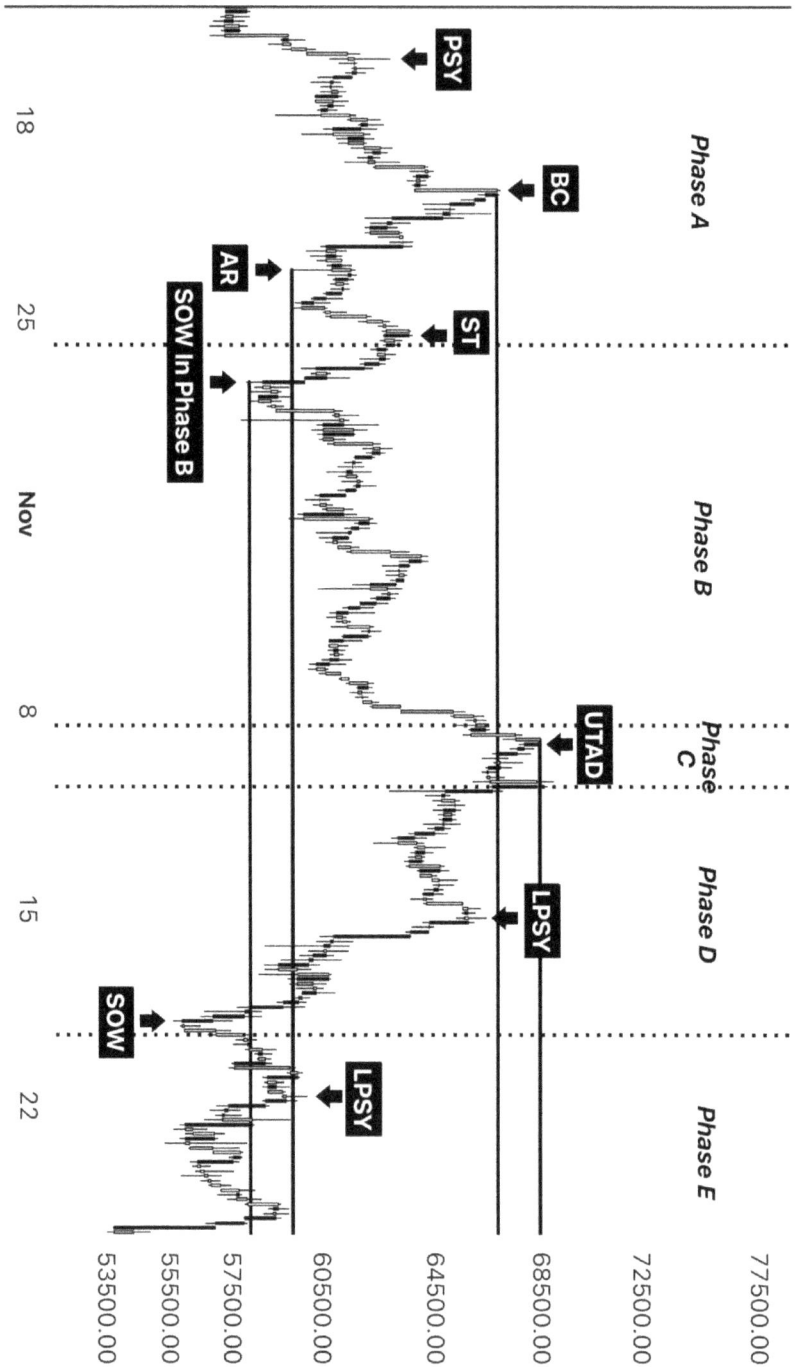

Fig. 99: *BTC/USDT H4 2021 (Oct/Nov) with Wyckoff distribution events and phases annotated.*

Preliminary Supply (PSY) - This is the point where substantial selling begins to emerge, often marked by increased volume and a halt in the price advance. PSY indicates that smart money is starting to distribute their positions in anticipation of a downward trend.

Buying Climax (BC) - The BC is a sharp increase in price followed by a sharp reversal. This event signals that buying pressure is exhausted, and supply is returning to the market. It typically occurs on high volume and marks a potential end of the uptrend.

Automatic Reaction (AR) - After the BC, the price experiences a strong decline due to increased supply. The AR creates a support level that acts as a reference point for future price action.

Secondary Test (ST) - Following the AR, the market may undergo a secondary test, in which the price advances towards the BC level but with lower volume. This indicates that buying pressure is waning and the stock is being distributed by strong hands.

Signs of Weakness (SOW) - These are bearish price and volume patterns that confirm distribution is taking place, such as increased volume on downswings and decreased volume on upswings, as well as on lower lows.

Upthrust After Distribution (UTAD) - The UTAD is a brief rally above the established resistance level of the trading range formed during Phase A or B. The purpose of the UTAD is to "trap" overconfident buyers who believe the market is breaking out to new highs. This event is usually accompanied by a decline in volume.

Last Point of Supply (LPSY) - The LPSY occurs after the UTAD and serves as a confirmation that the stock has been successfully distributed. The LPSY are weak rallies on low volume, indicating that there is little buying pressure left in the market.

To additionally determine if distribution is occurring, look for the following signs:

- Bearish volume (decreases on rallies, increases on declines
- Up-trending trendline broken
- Lower lows
- Lower Highs
- Stock weaker than the market (decreasing Relative Strength)

5. **Time your trade with the market**

Wait for the market to confirm markup or markdown with the Wyckoff cycle. Using technical methods to indicate a successful reversal in the markets (such as the S&P 500) is the signal to enter a trade with the movement of the markets.

The Wyckoff Method in summary details a 5-step method to following institutional investors "smart money" when selecting investments, and although it may take some practice to retroactively spot accumulations and distributions, the learning curve can be well worth the gain of an invaluable technical method.

Momentum Trading

Momentum trading is a strategy in which traders buy stocks that have exhibited strong upward or downward price movements in the recent past, with the expectation that these trends will continue. Momentum traders aim to profit from short-term price movements, often holding positions for only a few days or weeks.
Traders aim to enter long positions when the price is trending upwards and exit or short sell when the trend is downward. They will have strict risk management with regards to stop losses. Momentum traders typically rely on technical analysis and indicators to identify promising opportunities and manage risk. Several technical methods are commonly used to find and execute momentum trades:

Momentum Indicators:

Momentum traders will use momentum indicators to look for the most trending investments. Oscillators with overbought and oversold domains are particularly useful, as overbought indicates that momentum is strongly bullish on a stock or investment, whereas oversold indicates it is strongly bearish. Momentum traders will place trades with the momentum, so if the RSI for example is above 70, suggesting an investment is overbought, a momentum trader will buy the investment and sell when the investment is no longer overbought – i.e. that momentum is dissipating.

Follow The News:
News is perfect for bringing volatility into the markets and hence large price movements. This could be economic news such as an inflation rate release, and if the outcome is better or worse than expected plenty of momentum traders will be there to ride the wave. This could also be news of a natural disaster, such as the developments of Covid in 2020, a company bankruptcy, scandal or a company's earnings report. Momentum traders will keep up to date with what is hot and will look to trade there.

Breakouts and Breakdowns:
Momentum traders often look for breakouts or breakdowns from consolidation patterns, such as flags, pennants, triangles, and rectangles. Trading volume should be monitored during breakouts and breakdowns to confirm the strength of the move.

Trendlines and Channels:

Trendlines and channels help identify and visualize the direction of a trend. Trendlines connect the lows in an uptrend and the highs in a downtrend, while channels are formed by drawing parallel lines to the trendlines. Traders can use trendlines and channels to identify potential entry and exit points for momentum trades.

Contrarian Trading

Contrarian trading is a strategy in which traders take positions that are opposite to prevailing market trends or sentiment. Contrarian trading is inherently trickier than momentum trading because contrarian trades go against the market, which is often times correct.

Contrarian traders believe that markets often overreact to news and events, creating opportunities to profit from price reversals. This approach requires an understanding of market psychology and discipline to execute trades that may initially appear counterintuitive. Here are some of the best technical methods contrarian traders can use to identify trading opportunities:

Support and Resistance Levels:

Support and resistance levels are key price points where buying or selling pressure may increase, leading to potential reversals. Contrarian traders can use these levels to identify potential entry points for counter-trend trades. For example, when the price approaches a support level in a downtrend, contrarian traders might consider buying, anticipating a potential bounce.

Momentum Indicators:
Contrary to how momentum traders will use momentum indicators, contrarian traders will use these indicators to spot potential reversals when the market is overextended. For instance, when the RSI value is above 70 (overbought), a contrarian trader might consider selling or shorting the asset, expecting a price decline, rather than buying into the bullish momentum.

Divergences:
Divergences are a key part of contrarian trading, as divergences between price action and technical indicators, can signal potential trend reversals. A bullish divergence suggests weakening bearish momentum whereas a bearish divergence suggests weakening bullish momentum. The more indicators displaying a divergence within a given timeframe, the more likely a trend reversal is coming.

Sentiment Indicators:
Sentiment indicators, such as the Put/Call Ratio, the VIX, or the CNN Fear & Greed Index, can provide insights into the overall market sentiment. Contrarian traders can use these indicators to gauge when market sentiment is overly bullish or bearish and take positions that go against the prevailing sentiment.

Candlestick Patterns:

Candlestick patterns, such as the Hammer, Hanging Man, Doji, and Engulfing patterns, can help contrarian traders identify potential reversals in price trends. These patterns signal shifts in market psychology and can provide entry or exit points for counter-trend trades.

Fibonacci Retracement Levels:

Fibonacci retracement levels, derived from the Fibonacci sequence, are used to identify potential reversal points in a trend. Contrarian traders can use these levels (23.6%, 38.2%, 50%, 61.8%, and 78.6%) to anticipate potential counter-trend trades when the price retraces after a significant move.

Screening

Screening is a powerful tool that allows investors and traders to filter investments according to a specific criterion. Screeners gather all investments and attach a large range of data with each investment. The main types of data are financial data, such as a company's revenue and the P/E ratio, a simple ratio used for valuing a company's stock, and technical data such as the MACD. Technical data, unlike financial data, can apply to alternative investments such as commodities and currencies, giving traders a wider range of investments to choose from.

Traders can filter investments based on the overall technical rating, or the technical rating of specific indicators. For example, a trader could filter based on at least 15 of a basket of 20 technical indicators suggesting a 'strong buy'. A trader could also filter based on the RSI showing a 'strong buy' meaning a value above 70. A timeframe is also specified by the trader, and different timeframes will work best for different traders.

Short term traders will be more concerned with strong signals on the smaller timeframes when screening, whereas swing traders and long-term traders with the longer timeframes. Momentum traders may look to buy into investments that have strong buy signals, whilst contrarian traders will look to place contra-trend trades on these same investments – i.e., buy on a strong sell rating.

Screening investments can help narrow your choices down to a few candidate investments and take the heavy lifting associated with finding potential winners.

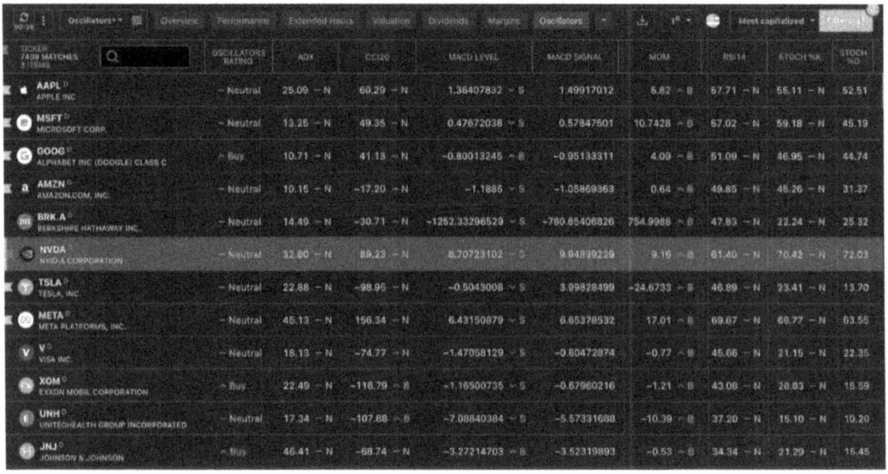

TICKER 7409 MATCHES	OSCILLATORS RATING	ADX	CCI20	MACD LEVEL	MACD SIGNAL	MOM	RSI14	STOCH %K	STOCH %D
AAPL APPLE INC	Neutral	25.09 N	60.29 N	1.36407832 S	1.49917012	5.82 B	57.71 N	55.11 N	52.51
MSFT MICROSOFT CORP.	Neutral	13.25 N	49.35 N	0.47672038 S	0.57847501	10.7428 B	57.02 N	59.18 N	45.19
GOOG ALPHABET INC (GOOGLE) CLASS C	Buy	10.71 N	41.13 N	−0.80013245 B	−0.95133311	4.09 B	51.09 N	46.95 N	44.74
AMZN AMAZON.COM, INC.	Neutral	10.15 N	−17.20 N	−1.1886 S	−1.05869363	0.64 B	49.85 N	45.26 N	31.37
BRK.A BERKSHIRE HATHAWAY INC.	Neutral	14.49 N	−30.71 N	−1252.33296529 S	−760.65406826	754.9986 B	47.83 N	22.24 N	25.32
NVDA NVIDIA CORPORATION	Neutral	32.80 N	89.23 N	8.70723102 S	9.94839229	9.16 B	61.40 N	70.42 N	72.03
TSLA TESLA, INC.	Neutral	22.88 N	−98.95 N	−0.5043008 S	3.99828499	−24.6733 B	46.89 N	23.41 N	13.70
META META PLATFORMS, INC.	Neutral	45.13 N	156.34 N	6.43150879 S	6.65378532	17.01 B	69.67 N	69.77 N	63.55
V VISA INC.	Neutral	18.13 N	−74.77 N	−1.47058129 S	−0.60472874	−0.77 B	45.66 N	21.15 N	22.35
XOM EXXON MOBIL CORPORATION	Buy	22.49 N	−118.79 B	−1.16500735 S	−0.67960216	−1.21 B	43.08 N	20.83 N	18.59
UNH UNITEDHEALTH GROUP INCORPORATED	Neutral	17.34 N	−107.88 B	−7.08840384 S	−5.57331688	−10.39 B	37.20 N	15.10 N	10.20
JNJ JOHNSON & JOHNSON	Buy	46.41 N	−68.74 N	−3.27214703 B	−3.52319893	−0.53 B	34.34 N	21.29 N	15.45

Fig. 100: *Stock screener from TradingView with display sorted by market cap.*

The screener used in this example came from tradingview.com and shows all U.S. companies sorted according to market cap. The screener shows how each stock is performing according to a wide variety of different oscillators, such as the MACD, RSI, Stochastic, ROC and a few other ones. We can sort according to the value of any of these technicals, so we can sort by RSI value for example and look for stocks that are the most oversold and overbought according to the RSI.

In an example for a swing trader trading on week to month long timeframes, trading on momentum, a reasonable screen (filter) would be the 50-day SMA < price, since this a quantifiable way of looking for investments that are trending bullish on the intermediate trend. For long-term investors, 200-day SMA < price may be more appropriate. A momentum trader may additionally screen for a variety of momentum indicators such as RSI > 70, MFI > 80 and so on. Applying the filters above would whittle the investments down to a small basket that an investor can analyze further and potentially trade from, as shown in a simplified table below.

Investment	Price	SMA-50	RSI	MFI
A	42.50	42.25	68	77
B	53.75	55.70	62	85
C	103.20	99.20	73	82
D	91.60	88.71	77	74
E	77.75	80.28	71	77

The filter set above would remove investments A,B,D,E from the table and just leave C for the trader's consideration. In reality, a filter this simple may leave many more investments, so a trader can tweak the criteria, or add filters such that the remaining selection is specific to the trader's needs.

Backtesting & Automated Trading

Backtesting is a technique used in trading to evaluate the performance of a trading strategy or system using historical data. The purpose of backtesting is to simulate how a trading strategy would have performed in the past, which can help traders to identify its strengths and weaknesses and refine the strategy for future use.

Backtesting involves analyzing historical market data and applying the rules of a trading strategy to that data to determine how the strategy would have performed. To perform a backtest, traders must first define the rules of their trading strategy, including entry and exit signals, stop-loss levels, position sizes and profit targets.

The main goal is to beat a buy and hold strategy (which is the performance of an investor who buys and holds an asset for the duration of the backtest) with an acceptable amount of risk.

Define your risk: The maximum dropdown is the maximum loss (risk) you are willing to take to make profits. If you are willing to lose up to 10% of your portfolio in trading, then your maximum dropdown of any strategy you use should be no larger than 10%. If it is, then you either need to reduce your position size or modify the strategy you are using.

Optimize Your Returns: Work on your strategy, test different values for indicators or use different ones to make your returns as high as possible for a given amount of risk.

It is also important to consider in the backtest the effects of any slippage on their trades (bid-ask spread) and any commission the broker takes from trades.

Once all is set, the rules are applied to historical market data, starting from a specific date, and moving forward in time. Entries and exits can be as simple as a limit order for an investment at a certain price, or when a single indicator crosses a certain value. Generally, for common strategies, such as an MA crossover or an oversold RSI, the trader does not need knowledge in coding, and various websites will allow you to easily backtest these but for more complex strategies with custom parameters, it may be necessary.

The results of a backtest can provide traders with valuable insights into the performance of their trading strategy. They can see how the strategy performed under different market conditions and identify areas where it could be improved. For example, how did a strategy based on momentum indicators perform in a bull market, a bear market, and a sideways market?

Traders can also backtest different strategies on different assets and see which strategies are optimal for each of the assets in question.

However, it is important to note that backtesting has limitations and is not a guarantee of future performance. Historical market data may not accurately reflect current market conditions, and backtesting cannot account for unpredictable events or external factors that may impact market performance.

Automated trading, also known as algorithmic trading or algo trading, takes backtesting one step further and involves using computer programs or algorithms to execute trading strategies automatically. These algorithms are typically designed to follow a set of predefined rules based on technical data. Automated trading has gained popularity in recent years due to advancements in technology and the increasing availability of trading platforms and tools. Automated trading does come with several benefits:

- **Emotionless trading** - Automated trading eliminates emotions from the decision-making process, reducing the impact of fear, greed, and other biases on trading decisions. This can lead to more disciplined and consistent trading performance.

- **Speed and efficiency** - Algorithms can execute trades at a much faster rate than humans, allowing traders to capitalize on short-term market opportunities more effectively. Automated systems can also process large volumes of data quickly, enabling more informed trading decisions.

- **Backtesting** - Automated trading systems can be backtested on historical data to evaluate their performance and optimize their parameters before being deployed in live markets.

- **24/7 trading** - Automated trading systems can operate around the clock, taking advantage of global market opportunities without requiring constant human intervention.

Automated trading does come with some drawbacks, the main one currently is system failure risk. Like any technology, automated trading systems can experience technical issues, such as hardware or software failures, which could lead to missed trading opportunities or unexpected losses. This means that they will require constant monitoring to ensure systems are working as they should be, and like backtesting, may require coding knowledge to diagnose any issues with the algorithm. Additionally, when it comes to trading, sometimes a human touch actually improves the outcomes – particularly when you get good at trading. You develop a deeper feeling for the assets that you trade, and you heuristically pick up repeating price action that you then use in your analysis and, hence trading decisions. In this way, using automated trading can for some people, see better use as another piece of evidence in your analysis rather than a straight up buy or sell signal.

ADVANCED TECHNICAL CONCEPTS & TRADING STRATEGIES
KEY POINTS:

- **Cycles are repeating patterns and trends exhibited on the markets. Examples include the business cycle, Kondratieff waves and the presidential cycle.**

- **The Elliott Wave theory stipulates that price moves in a series of 5 impulse waves followed by 3 corrective waves. These can be exhibited on any timeframe, and traders can use them to guide trading activity.**

- **The Wyckoff Method outlines 5 steps to stock selection and how to identify periods of accumulation and distribution to best profit from the markets.**

- **Screening is a tool used to filter investments by technical and financial data.**

- **Backtesting involves testing a strategy against historical price data to see how it may perform. Automated trading takes a strategy and automatically executes trades on your behalf.**

VII. Market Psychology

Market psychology looks at how investors emotions, biases and social factors influence their decision-making process. This psychology, studied professionally as behavioral finance, explains phenomena such as asset bubbles that doesn't conform to traditional financial belief, chiefly in the efficient market hypothesis (EMH). The EMH states that all known information is already priced into the markets and that price moves reflect this known information. In this way, no-one is able to make superior risk-adjusted returns from the market.

The EMH, while studies have often found it to be true in many circumstances, has been controversial and has failed to explain numerous market phenomena, such as asset bubbles. Complete rationality by market participants is largely known to be not the case, as we will see in a later case study, and the understanding of how emotion and psychology affects the markets has seen growing importance in investors and industry professionals.

This market psychology is studied in behavioral finance, a study within behavioral economics, which challenges the rationality assumed in traditional finance and postulates that investors and market participants are not always rational humans, and that emotions and biases play a part in determining the supply and demand in the markets.

This emotion, that includes hope, greed, excitement, fear, regret, anxiety, and panic, can often cause prices to deviate from what may seem fundamentally reasonable, and can lead to stock market bubbles and crashes.

Collectively, these emotion and biases feed into market sentiment, which is the investors views on the state of the markets.

Bullish market sentiments are when there are more positive feelings about the markets, more hope, more greed, more excitement and what typically results are riskier investor behavior. There is more speculation and market prices tend to rise above the fundamental value of the companies and assets being invested into.

On the contrary, bearish market sentiment involves fear, panic and anxiety and market prices can be left a discount from their fundamental value. There is more caution in the markets, and investors are quick to take any profits on small pumps in price.

Psychological Biases

Loss Aversion & The Disposition Effect

Quite possibly the most important concepts to understand as an investor yourself, loss aversion is a concept where investors feel the pain of losses more than the pleasure of gains. A practical manifestation attributable to loss aversion is the disposition effect. The disposition effect is a phenomenon where investors tend to hold onto losing investments for too long and sell winning investments too quickly. It is a cognitive bias that can result in suboptimal investment decisions and can lead to lower returns and higher risks.

The disposition effect occurs because investors tend to focus on the gains or losses of an investment rather than its potential future performance. They feel the pain of losses more acutely than the pleasure of gains, which leads them to hold onto losing investments in the hope of breaking even or avoiding further losses. On the other hand, they tend to sell winning investments too quickly to lock in profits, even if there is potential for further gains.

In a famous example of the disposition effect in practice, a group of people are given two scenarios, each with two possible options.

	Option A	Option B
Scenario 1	50% chance of a $1000 gain, 50% chance of a $0 gain.	100% chance of a $500 gain.
Scenario 2	50% chance of a $1000 loss, 50% chance of a $0 loss.	100% chance of a $500 loss.

In scenario 1, most people chose option B, but in scenario 2, most people chose option A. Notice how statistically, both option A and option B have the same value in both scenarios, yet the results in choosing the options was wildly different. The implications of the disposition effect within investing means that one may be tempted to take profits prematurely, or to reposition a stop loss. This behavior alters the risk to reward of a trade, often reducing it (making the trade riskier). It also negatively impacts an investor through opportunity, where holding losing trades for longer means that throughout that duration, the investor is missing the opportunity to make a profitable trade elsewhere.

By understanding this bias, investors should look to keep their trading methodical by following technical analysis methods and refraining from acting on a hunch. If a trade is initially profitable, but the price pulls backs towards breakeven, then it is often best to leave it, regardless of the nail-biting urge to close it in the green. Similarly, if you are convinced of a trade, such as a breakout from a pattern, but the price heads towards your stop-loss, then again it is best to leave it and resist the urge to move the stop loss further because of your conviction to the success to the trade.

Confirmation Bias

Confirmation bias is the tendency for investors to seek out and pay more attention to information that confirms their pre-existing beliefs while ignoring or dismissing information that contradicts those beliefs. This bias can have several negative impacts on investors and their decision-making processes:

Overconfidence: Confirmation bias can lead to overconfidence in investment decisions, as investors may believe that their analysis and predictions are more accurate than they are. This overconfidence can result in taking on excessive risk or not adequately diversifying their investments.

Poor decision-making: By focusing primarily on information that supports their beliefs, investors may overlook important contradictory data or alternative viewpoints, leading to suboptimal investment decisions.

Resistance to change: Confirmation bias can make investors resistant to changing their opinions or strategies, even when new information suggests that they should. This rigidity can lead to holding onto losing positions or missing out on profitable opportunities.

To overcome confirmation bias, investors can adopt several strategies:

Actively seek out contradictory information: Make a conscious effort to research and consider information that challenges your beliefs and investment decisions. This can help you gain a more balanced perspective and make more informed choices.

Be open to alternative viewpoints: Encourage open discussions with friends, colleagues, or advisors who have different investment opinions. Engaging in constructive debates can help expose blind spots and lead to more well-rounded decision-making.

Herd Mentality

Herd mentality is the inclination for investors to follow the actions of the majority, rather than making independent decisions based on their analysis. This can lead to investment bubbles and crashes, as investors may buy into overvalued assets or sell undervalued assets simply because others are doing so. Herd mentality can result in suboptimal investment decisions and increased risk.

For example, basing investment decisions solely on what influencers may say about an investment is regarded as herd mentality.

Time Series Biases

- **Weekdays –** of all the weekdays, Mondays by far are the worst performing trading day, with Fridays narrowly being the best.

- **Januarys** – Januarys are normally the best performing month throughout the year. The reasoning for this seems attributable to investors tax-loss harvesting before the new year starts, as well as Christmas bonuses being invested into the markets.

- **November-April** – This 6-month period consistently outperforms by a wide margin the May-October period, giving rise to the saying "Sell in May and go away" or the "Halloween Strategy".

- **Holiday Effect** – The final trading day prior to a holiday has generated higher returns.

Sentiment Indicators

Sentiment indicators typically show how bullish or bearish investor behavior is and can be used alongside technical indicators in determining the trend.

Market sentiment can give investors buy and sell signals in varying ways and gives an overview of the state of the markets. The most common market sentiment indicators include:

VIX – Volatility Index

The VIX represents the market's confidence in the short-term price changes for the S&P 500 Index. The volatility shows how fast prices change, and so higher volatility means less confidence in the short-term price and therefore higher risk, and an implied greater fear amongst investors.

The VIX therefore measures market sentiment, as shown in Fig. 101. The higher the value of the VIX, the greater the fear in the market. Here, we can see that during the Covid crash of 2020, the VIX closely follows the inverse of the S&P 500 index.

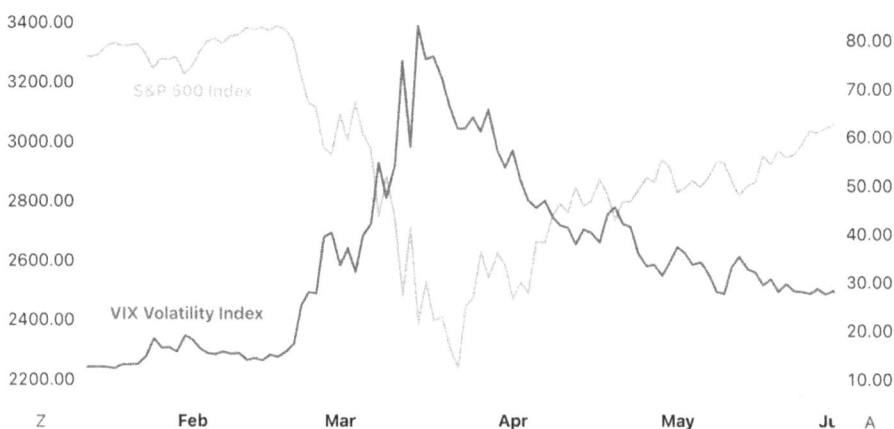

Fig. 101: *The CBOE Volatility Index (VIX) relative to the S&P 500 Index during 2020's stock market crash.*

The VIX works by deriving its value from option prices. In times of uncertainty for the future, investors more often hedge their trades with countertrades. For example, if an investor placed a long position on a stock, they might place a put option to hedge against their long position. The number of put options increases as there is uncertainty and since the VIX compares the ratio between the S&P 500 to the number of put options in the market, the VIX goes up when the number of put options increases.

The VIX, as demonstrated in Fig. 101, follows an inverse of the S&P 500 around 80% of the time. Therefore, quite regularly, you will see the VIX move in tandem with the S&P 500. These moves in tandem are often short-lived but if they do last a day or longer, they can give valuable insight into market sentiment. If the S&P 500 is moving up, but the VIX is also increasing, investors are anticipating bearish news ahead. If the S&P 500 is falling but the VIX is also falling, then investors are optimistic about the future.

A VIX below 20 is regarded as bullish sentiment (greed) in the markets and a VIX above 30 is regarded as fear in the markets. In most recessions, the value of the VIX surpasses 50 at least once, therefore this fact can be checked when a recession is suspected. If the VIX has not yet reached 50, and evidence points to a recession, then this is a likely indicator for worse to come in the stock market.

The VIX can also be bought as an ETF or derivative investment by itself and when used this way, is a good alternative way to short the U.S. stock market.

The VIX can also be used in a similar way to other technical indicators such as confirming breakouts and spotting divergences. It is particularly useful when compared with the S&P 500 Index, which in turn is an important index to monitor when trading stocks, since the majority of stocks move with the market.

Remember that for most sentiment indicators discussed here, diverging lines is actually the normal healthy relationship between price and indicator, and trendlines moving in the same direction is the red flag.

In Fig. 102, the bullish trend on the SPX is confirmed by the falling VIX. The bullish trend ends with the price breaking below the line of support, which is confirmed by the VIX breaking above the line of resistance on the same trading day.

Fig. 102: *S&P 500 (SPX) vs. CBOE Volatility Index (VIX) H4 2022 (Sep-Dec) with respective trendlines annotated and breakouts circled.*

In Fig. 103, we see that the SPX is in a bearish trend, but so is the VIX, as we can see from both trendlines heading a bearish direction. The SPX is bearish, yet the implication of the VIX is bullish...

This is a sign that something will correct this relationship in the near future, whether it's the VIX breaking its trendline and heading up, confirming the bearish price action in the SPX or the SPX breaking above its trendline and confirming the bullish implication of the VIX. Fortunately for the bulls, the latter ends up happening!

Fig. 103: *S&P 500 (SPX) vs. CBOE Volatility Index (VIX) H1 2023 (Feb-Mar)*

Put/Call Ratio

The put-call ratio is a widely used sentiment indicator that compares the trading volume of put options (bearish bets) to call options (bullish bets) in the options market. A high put-call ratio indicates that there are more put options being traded, suggesting a bearish sentiment, while a low ratio indicates a higher number of call options being traded, suggesting a bullish sentiment. Extreme values in the put-call ratio can signal potential market reversals, as excessive pessimism or optimism may be a contrarian indicator.

Fig. 104: *S&P 500 (SPX) on top vs. Put/Call Ratio (PC) on the bottom D1 2022-2023 (Aug-Mar) with extreme PC reading annotated.*

In Fig. 104, the PC reading spikes to a multi-month high at the end of December, indicating extreme bearish sentiment at this point. Despite the dire sentiment, the SPX begins a rally soon after, with the PC spike signaling the low within a correction in a bullish trend – a perfect contrarian signal.

The Put/Call Ratio may also be used in ways described for other technical indicators, such as for identifying trendlines and patterns and confirming those on the price.

In Fig. 105, another example of the SPX, as the price of the SPX slowly increases, the PC slowly declines, and the divergence indicates a normal relationship. However, a keen eye would notice some form of falling wedge on the PC, and the subsequent breakout of the PC as the SPX enters a triangle pattern. The PC breakout is not an immediate sell, but when the SPX breaks down from the triangle pattern, the falling wedge on the PC confirms this price breakdown and should add conviction to the trade.

Fig. 105: *S&P 500 (SPX) on top vs. Put/Call Ratio (PC) on the bottom H4 2022-2023 (Dec-Mar) with trendlines annotated.*

Fear & Greed Index

The fear and greed index is not a single indicator, rather a compilation of several indicators to measure investor fear and greed in the markets.

If you do an internet search for fear and greed index, you should get some good results from popular financial websites that all may have unique methodologies of determining fear and greed. They typically include a mix of the VIX or a variation of it, economic indicators or specific indicators that correlate with (lack of) risk investors are willing to take.

Some examples of indicators of risk-taking activity includes the number of junk bonds purchased. Junk bonds are a speculative high interest paying bonds, that are at high risk of default.

The underlying premise of the fear-greed index is that in times of greed, investors take more risk than in times of fear.

In each case, the value is between 0-100, 0 being extreme fear and 100 being extreme greed. The implication here is that in times of extreme fear, the market price could be undervalued to its true price and could be a good buy opportunity. In times of extreme greed, the markets could be overheating and could indicate a good exit point.

Open Interest & Short Interest

Open interest refers to the number of outstanding contracts or positions in a particular market or asset. It is an important metric for investors and traders who are looking to assess market sentiment and identify potential trading opportunities.

Open interest is often used in the context of futures and options contracts, where it represents the total number of outstanding contracts that have not been settled or closed out. For example, if there are 100 open futures contracts for a particular asset, it means that there are 100 investors who currently hold positions in that asset and have not yet closed their positions.

Open interest can be used to gauge market sentiment and identify potential trends. For example, if open interest is increasing for a particular asset, it may indicate that more investors are entering the market and taking positions in that asset, which could be a sign of bullish sentiment. Conversely, if open interest is decreasing, it may indicate that investors are exiting the market and taking profits, which could be a sign of bearish sentiment.

Open interest can also be used to identify potential trading opportunities. For example, if open interest is increasing for a particular asset, it may indicate that there is a high level of demand for that asset, which could create opportunities for traders to enter long positions. Conversely, if open interest is decreasing, it may indicate that there is a high level of supply for that asset, which could create opportunities for traders to enter short positions.

Short interest is a near opposite of open interest and refers to the total number of shares of a publicly traded company that have been sold short but have not yet been closed out or covered by the short sellers. In other words, it is the number of shares currently borrowed by short sellers who are betting that the stock price will decline.

A high or increasing short interest relative to the total number of outstanding shares (known as the short interest ratio) can indicate a bearish sentiment towards the stock, as it suggests that many investors believe the stock price will decline. Conversely, a low or decreasing short interest ratio can signal bullish sentiment.

Stocks with high short interest may be susceptible to short squeezes. When a stock with high short interest experiences a significant price increase, short sellers may be forced to cover their positions by buying back the shares, which can create additional buying pressure and push the stock price even higher. This phenomenon is known as a short squeeze and can lead to rapid and significant price gains, such as GameStop (GME) in 2021.

Case Study - The Dot-Com Bubble

There are few better examples of the full array of market psychology at play than the dot-com bubble of the early 21st century.

In 1999, at a point that the internet was near certain to change the future and companies were spawning in their masses to try and capitalize on this company. Computers had changed from a luxury good to a necessity thanks to the internet and now the stage was ripe for companies to add value to the internet that most U.S. and European households now had access to. Companies that had a .com extension on their name were seen as desirable and the market price for these companies began to rise.

The NASDAQ Composite Index that includes the largest technology companies, quadrupled from around 1250 points in March 1997, to 5000 points in March 2000.

Webvan was one of the companies to fall in the dot com crash, it declared bankruptcy in 2001, 3 years after starting up. The company offered home delivery of groceries and attempted to scale fast to gain a competitive advantage over other similar start-ups.

Webvan successfully raised $396 million through venture capital firms, and later IPO-ed in November 1999, where the company was valued at $4.8 billion. In reality, up until that point, the company had generated just $395,000 in revenue.

Taking Webvan's Q4 1999 financials and comparing the ratios to the tech sector today, it seems that nothing makes sense. But the price of Webvan continued to rise amidst speculation, hype, and investor FOMO (fear of missing out).

Something would finally topple the first domino in March 2000, as Japan declared a recession and a global sell-off of stocks ensued. The stock market turned in the other direction, a foreign announcement of a recession was enough to turn the the tides. Once started, the sell-off cannot be stopped and other once euphoric investors also start selling their positions. The bubble was officially burst, and the decline continues, with NASDAQ Composite halving in value in just 3 months after its peak in March 2000. Webvan subsequently lost 99% of its value a year after its peak in March 2000.

But why?

The company's financials have dropped but not enough to warrant such a drastic decline in value. The company's business model was not great in hindsight, but it has not changed since a time when the stock price was soaring. The competitive advantage is still there. A Japanese recession and increased interest rates could moderately affect the company due to large amount of debt, but again, the company had a similar level of debt prior to the crash. The main thing that changed was the investor appetite for risk – the market sentiment. There was greed, FOMO and a whole range of hype driving up the market prices irrationally. All it took was one macroeconomic event that started the domino effect, and market sentiment changed from greed to fear at the flick of a switch. Webvan lost almost $3 billion in market cap in 2020, but its fundamentals have not changed that much.

Along with the indicators, the sentiment of investors during the dot-com bubble and other asset bubbles would have been a telltale sign to a smart investor that things started to get overheated and to get out the markets.

The emotions during the market cycle of the bubble would have looked like the following:

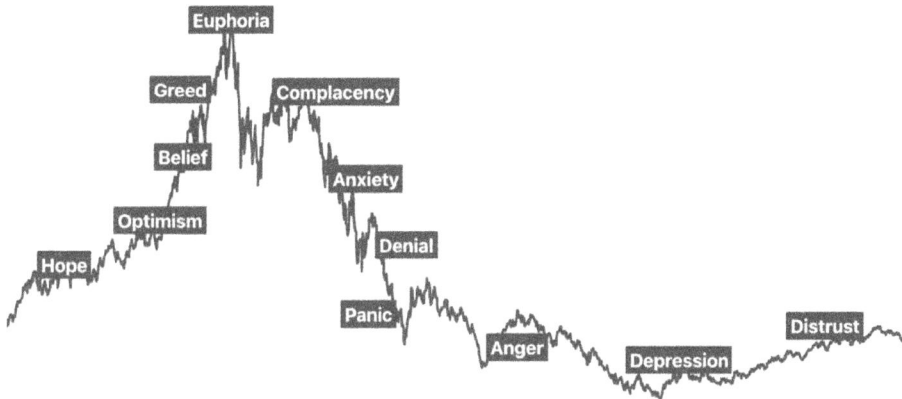

Fig. 106: *Various plausible emotions at different stages of a stock market bubble. The emotions are laid on the NASDAQ 100 Index between 1998 and 2004.*

- **Hope –** 'There's a possibility that these internet companies could go up'.

- **Optimism –** 'This bullish trend is real; these internet companies are next big thing'.

- **Belief –** 'I am moving my savings into these internet stocks'.

- **Greed –** 'If I would have put my children's college fund in, I would have been a millionaire already'.

- **Euphoria –** 'I am rich'. 'I am on top of the world'.

- **Complacency** – 'Just a healthy, temporary dip in price – I know what I am doing'. 'Do not sell, just hold'. 'I am taking advantage of the dip and buying more'.

- **Anxiety** – 'These internet stocks are dipping longer than I thought, I may be overinvested'.

- **Denial** – 'I have chosen solid investments'. 'It cannot go down more'.

- **Panic** – 'It is over. I am selling everything. You should do the same'.

- **Anger** – 'How could this happen? These internet companies are trash'. "How could the government allow this?'

- **Depression** – 'I lost all my savings. I could have sold at the top and doubled my money. I could have sold there or there and lost less money'.

- **Distrust** – 'Just a fake pump in price'.

Notice how the best buying opportunities would be when the mood is lowest, and the worst buying opportunities would have been when the mood was the highest.

The market is often irrational, and when price does not reflect the value of the company in the short to mid-term, then it is likely driven by emotion.

"Be fearful when others are greedy, be greedy when others are fearful".

MARKET PSYCHOLOGY
KEY POINTS:

- *Emotion and psychological biases can adversely affect investment and trading decisions and cause irrationality in the markets. These include loss aversion, confirmation bias and herd mentality.*

- *Market sentiment indicators show investors overall attitude to the markets and can be used much in the same way as technical indicators.*

- *Growing risky behavior is generally a bullish sign, and lessening risky behavior is generally a bearish sign.*

- *Different parts of an asset bubble cycle come with different emotions.*

VIII. Glossary

- **Accumulation** - The process of buying an asset over an extended period of time.

- **Accumulation / Distribution Line** - A technical analysis indicator that uses volume and price data to measure buying and selling pressure.

- **Advance/Decline Line (A/D Line)** - A technical indicator that tracks the net number of advancing stocks minus the net number of declining stocks.

- **Algorithmic Trading** - A method of trading using computer programs that execute trades based on predetermined rules and parameters.

- **Ascending Triangle** - A bullish chart pattern that forms when the price is making higher lows and a horizontal resistance level is being tested.

- **Backtesting** - The process of evaluating a trading strategy by testing it against historical price data.

- **Bar Chart -** A type of chart used in technical analysis that displays the open, high, low, and close prices of an asset over a given time period.

- **Bear Market** - A bear market is a financial market characterized by falling asset prices and a generally pessimistic sentiment among investors.

- **Bearish -** A term used to describe a market or asset that is expected to decline in value.

- **Bearish Divergence –** Also negative divergence, a technical analysis term that occurs when an asset's price makes a new high or low, but the corresponding technical indicator fails to confirm the trend, indicating potential weakness in the market.

- **Bollinger Bands -** A technical indicator that measures volatility by plotting two standard deviations above and below a moving average.

- **Breadth Indicators -** Technical analysis indicators that measure the participation of stocks or other assets in a trend or market move.

- **Breakout -** A technical analysis term that refers to a price move above or below a significant level of support or resistance.

- **Bull Market -** A bull market is a financial market characterized by rising asset prices and a generally optimistic sentiment among investors.

- **Bullish -** A term used to describe a market or asset that is expected to increase in value.

- **Bullish Divergence –** Bullish divergence is a technical analysis term that refers to a pattern where an asset's price is making lower lows, but the corresponding technical indicator is making higher lows.

- **Buy Signal -** A technical analysis term that refers to a signal that indicates a potential buying opportunity.

- **Candlestick Chart -** A type of chart used in technical analysis that displays the open, high, low, and close prices of an asset, similar to a bar chart.

- **Channel -** A technical analysis term that refers to the range of prices that an asset trades within over a given time period, bounded by two parallel trendlines.

- **Chart Pattern -** A recognizable pattern that appears on a price chart and is used by technical analysts to predict future price movements.

- **Consolidation -** Consolidation is a technical analysis term used to describe a period of time in which an asset's price trades within a narrow range, typically after a period of significant price movement.

- **Correction -** A temporary decline in the price of an asset, often after a period of strong growth, that is considered a normal and healthy part of a longer-term uptrend.

- **Cup and Handle -** A bullish continuation pattern that forms after a period of consolidation, in which the price of the asset forms a U-shaped "cup" and then a smaller "handle" before breaking out to the upside.

- **Day Trading -** A trading strategy in which positions are opened and closed within the same trading day, often using technical analysis to identify short-term price movements.

- **Death Cross -** A technical analysis term that occurs when a short-term moving average crosses below a long-term moving average, indicating a potential shift in the market trend to the downside.

- **Descending Triangle -** A bearish chart pattern that forms when the price is making lower highs and a horizontal support level is being tested.

- **Distribution -** A technical analysis term that refers to the process of selling an asset, usually by institutional investors or market makers, in order to take profits or reduce exposure to a particular asset.

- **Divergence -** A technical analysis term that occurs when the price of an asset is moving in the opposite direction of a related indicator, such as an oscillator or moving average.

- **Doji -** A candlestick pattern that occurs when the opening and closing prices of an asset are very close or the same, indicating indecision in the market.

- **Double Bottom -** A bullish chart pattern that forms when the price tests a support level twice and bounces back up, signaling a potential reversal in the market trend.

- **Double Top -** A technical chart pattern that signals a potential trend reversal. This pattern occurs when the price of an asset reaches a high level, then pulls back, and then returns to the same high level again before declining.

- **Dow Theory –** The Dow Theory is a technical analysis methodology that uses market trends and price movements to provide insights into the overall health of the economy and potential changes in the market.

- **Down Trend -** A technical analysis term that refers to a consistent pattern of declining prices over a specific period of time.

- **Elliott Wave -** A technical analysis theory that suggests that financial markets move in predictable cycles and can be divided into five wave patterns, with three waves in the direction of the trend and two waves against the trend.

- **Engulfing Pattern -** A bullish or bearish candlestick pattern that occurs when a smaller candlestick is completely engulfed by a larger candlestick, indicating a potential trend reversal.

- **Exponential Moving Average (EMA) -** A technical analysis tool that places more weight on recent price data, resulting in a more responsive moving average that is more sensitive to short-term price movements.

- **False Breakout (Fakeout) -** A technical analysis term that occurs when the price of an asset appears to break through a significant level of support or resistance, but then quickly reverses direction and returns to the previous range.

- **Fear and Greed Index -** A sentiment indicator that measures the level of fear or greed in the market, based on factors such as volatility, trading volume, and investor sentiment.

- **Fibonacci Retracement -** A technical analysis tool that uses horizontal lines to indicate potential levels of support or resistance at the key Fibonacci levels, based on the mathematical relationships between numbers in the Fibonacci sequence.

- **Flag and Pennant -** A technical chart pattern that signals a potential continuation in the current market trend. The flag pattern consists of a sharp price move followed by a period of consolidation in the form of a rectangular shape, while the pennant pattern is similar but has a triangular shape.

- **Gap -** A technical analysis term that occurs when the price of an asset moves sharply up or down with no trading activity between the previous closing price and the new opening price.

- **Golden Cross -** A technical analysis term that occurs when a short-term moving average crosses above a long-term moving average, indicating a potential shift in the market trend to the upside.

- **Hammer -** A bullish candlestick pattern that occurs when the price of an asset opens near the low of the day and closes near the high of the day, with a long lower shadow. This pattern indicates potential buying pressure and a possible trend reversal.

- **Hanging Man -** A bearish candlestick pattern that is similar to the hammer pattern, but occurs after a significant uptrend and signals potential selling pressure and a possible trend reversal.

- **Head and Shoulders -** A bearish chart pattern that signals a potential trend reversal. This pattern is formed by a peak (the head) with two smaller peaks (the shoulders) on either side, with a neckline that connects the low points between the shoulders.

- **Heikin-Ashi -** A type of chart used in technical analysis that uses candlesticks to represent price movement, but incorporates a modified formula for calculating open, high, low, and close prices, resulting in a smoother chart that is less affected by short-term fluctuations.

- **High-Low Index -** A technical analysis tool that measures the ratio of new highs to new lows in the market, used to identify potential trends or reversals.

- **Index -** A benchmark that measures the performance of a group of assets or a particular market, often used for comparison or tracking purposes.

- **Indicator -** A technical analysis tool that uses mathematical calculations and/or visual representations to identify

potential trends, momentum, or levels of support and
resistance in the market.

-   **Inverse Head and Shoulders** - A bullish chart pattern that
    is the opposite of the head and shoulders pattern. This
    pattern is formed by two troughs (the shoulders) with a
    lower trough (the head) in between, with a neckline that
    connects the high points between the shoulders. A break
    above the neckline indicates a potential shift in the market
    trend to the upside.

-   **Leverage** - The use of borrowed funds or financial
    instruments to increase the potential return or risk of an
    investment, often used in trading and speculation.

-   **Limit Order** - A type of order in which a trader specifies the
    maximum or minimum price at which they are willing to buy
    or sell an asset, often used to control the price at which a
    trade is executed.

-   **Line Chart** - A type of chart used in technical analysis that
    displays the price movement of an asset as a continuous
    line, often used to identify long-term trends or patterns.

-   **Liquidity** - The degree to which an asset can be bought or
    sold quickly and easily in the market, without affecting its
    price or trading volume.

-   **Long Position** - A trading position in which a trader buys
    an asset with the expectation that its price will increase,
    resulting in a profit when the asset is sold at a higher price.

-   **MACD (Moving Average Convergence Divergence)** - A
    technical analysis indicator that uses two moving averages
    and a signal line to identify potential changes in momentum
    and trend direction in the market.

- **Margin -** The amount of money or collateral that a trader must deposit with a broker in order to open and maintain a trading position, often used to increase leverage and potential returns or losses.

- **Market Cap -** The total value of a company's outstanding shares of stock, calculated by multiplying the current share price by the number of outstanding shares.

- **Market Order -** A market order is a type of order to buy or sell a financial asset at the current market price. When a market order is placed, the order is executed immediately, and the investor or trader receives the best available price for the asset.

- **Mean Reversion -** A technical analysis theory that suggests that asset prices tend to revert to their mean or average over time, after experiencing periods of deviation or volatility.

- **Momentum -** A technical analysis term that refers to the speed or rate of change of an asset's price, often used to identify potential shifts in the market trend or direction.

- **Money Flow Index (MFI) -** A technical analysis indicator that uses both price and volume data to identify potential trends or reversals in the market.

- **Morning Star -** A bullish candlestick pattern that occurs after a significant downtrend, consisting of a long red candlestick, followed by a short or long doji, followed by a long green candlestick. This pattern indicates potential buying pressure and a possible trend reversal.

- **Moving Average -** A technical analysis tool that calculates the average price of an asset over a specific period of time, often used to identify trends or levels of support and resistance.

- **On-Balance Volume (OBV)** - A technical analysis indicator that uses volume data to identify potential trends or reversals in the market, based on the idea that buying and selling pressure can be inferred from changes in volume.

- **Open Interest** - The total number of outstanding options or futures contracts for a particular asset, often used to identify potential levels of support and resistance or to gauge market sentiment.

- **Oscillator** - A technical analysis tool that uses a mathematical formula to measure the momentum or trend strength of an asset, often used to identify potential overbought or oversold conditions in the market.

- **Overbought** - A technical analysis term that occurs when an asset's price has risen too quickly and is likely to experience a correction or pullback in the near future.

- **Oversold** - A technical analysis term that occurs when an asset's price has fallen too quickly and is likely to experience a rebound or recovery in the near future.

- **Pennant** - A bullish or bearish chart pattern that occurs when a period of consolidation is followed by a continuation of the previous trend, often resembling a small triangle or flag shape.

- **Price Action** - A technical analysis approach that focuses on the movement and behavior of an asset's price, often used to identify potential patterns or trends in the market.

- **Price Target -** A predetermined price level or exit point for a trading position, often used to lock in profits or manage risk.

- **Range -** A technical analysis term that refers to the difference between an asset's highest and lowest price levels during a particular period of time, often used to identify potential levels of support and resistance in the market.

- **Rate of Change (ROC) -** A technical analysis indicator that uses a formula based on the percentage change in an asset's price over a specific period of time, to identify potential trends or momentum changes in the market.

- **Relative Strength -** Relative Strength is a technical analysis term that measures the strength of one asset relative to another asset or to the broader market. It is calculated by dividing the price of one asset by the price of another asset or by an index, and plotting the resulting ratio over time.

- **Relative Strength Index (RSI) -** A technical analysis indicator that uses a formula based on the ratio of average gains to average losses over a specific period of time, to identify potential overbought or oversold conditions in the market.

- **Resistance -** A technical analysis term that refers to a price level or zone at which an asset's price is likely to encounter selling pressure, often used as a potential exit point for short positions or a potential entry point for long positions.

- **Retracement -** A temporary reversal or correction in an asset's price movement, often used to identify potential buying opportunities in an uptrend or potential selling opportunities in a downtrend.

- **Risk Management -** The process of identifying, assessing, and controlling potential risks associated with trading or investing, often used to minimize potential losses and maximize potential gains.

- **Risk-To-Reward -** A calculation used to assess the potential risk and reward of a trading position, often used to determine the optimal position size or to evaluate the potential profitability of a trading strategy.

- **Short Selling -** A trading strategy in which a trader borrows and sells an asset with the expectation that its price will decrease, and buys back the asset at a lower price to make a profit.

- **Stochastic Oscillator -** A technical analysis indicator that uses a formula based on the relationship between an asset's closing price and its price range over a specific period of time, to identify potential overbought or oversold conditions in the market.

- **Stop-Loss Order -** A type of order in which a trader specifies a price level or range at which a position should be automatically closed in order to limit potential losses.

- **Support -** A technical analysis term that refers to a price level or zone at which an asset's price is likely to encounter buying pressure, often used as a potential entry point for long positions or a potential exit point for short positions.

- **Swing Trading -** A trading strategy in which positions are held for a period of several days to several weeks, often based on short-term technical analysis or momentum indicators.

- **Symmetrical Triangle -** A chart pattern that occurs when an asset's price is moving within a narrowing range, often resembling a triangle shape, and indicating potential uncertainty or indecision in the market.

- **Take Profit -** A predetermined price level or exit point for a trading position, often used to lock in profits or manage risk.

- **Technical Analysis -** The study of past market data, including price and volume, to identify potential patterns, trends, and indicators that may be used to make trading decisions and manage risk.

- **Technical Indicator -** A mathematical formula or chart pattern used in technical analysis to identify potential trends or changes in the market.

- **Timeframe** - The period of time over which market data is analyzed, often ranging from minutes to years, and used to identify potential trends or patterns in the market.

- **Trading Plan -** A comprehensive strategy for trading or investing, including specific entry and exit points, risk management guidelines, and other relevant information.

- **Trend -** A technical analysis term that refers to the general direction of an asset's price movement over a specific period of time, often used to identify potential buying or selling opportunities in the market.

- **Trendline -** A straight line drawn on a chart that connects two or more points, often used to identify potential levels of support or resistance and to visualize trends in the market.

- **Triple Bottom -** Triple Bottom is a bullish chart pattern that occurs when an asset's price reaches a certain level of support three times without breaking through, indicating potential buying pressure and a possible trend reversal.

- **Triple Top -** A bearish chart pattern that occurs when an asset's price reaches a certain level of resistance three times without breaking through, indicating potential selling pressure and a possible trend reversal.

- **VIX -** The CBOE Volatility Index, a measure of the implied volatility of the S&P 500 index options, often used as a gauge of market sentiment and potential trend changes.

- **Volatility -** A statistical measure of the variability or dispersion of an asset's price over time, often used to identify potential risk and to manage trading strategies and positions.

- **Volume -** The total number of shares or contracts traded during a particular period of time, often used to analyze market activity and potential trend changes.

- **Weighted Moving Average (WMA)** - A technical analysis indicator that assigns greater weight to more recent price data, often used to identify potential trend changes and to calculate other technical indicators.

- **Whipsaw -** A technical analysis term that refers to a situation in which an asset's price moves in one direction and then immediately reverses, often causing traders to incur losses or miss potential trading opportunities.

- **Wyckoff Method -** A technical analysis method that uses price and volume data to identify potential accumulation or distribution patterns in the market, often used to make trading decisions and manage risk.

www.ingramcontent.com/pod-product-compliance
Lightning Source LLC
Chambersburg PA
CBHW071202210326
41597CB00016B/1637